Guardian Angels

Guardian Angels

*Discover the world of angels
and how to communicate
with your guardian angel*

Hazel Whitaker and
Cynthia Blanche

PB

PARKGATE
BOOKS

Contents

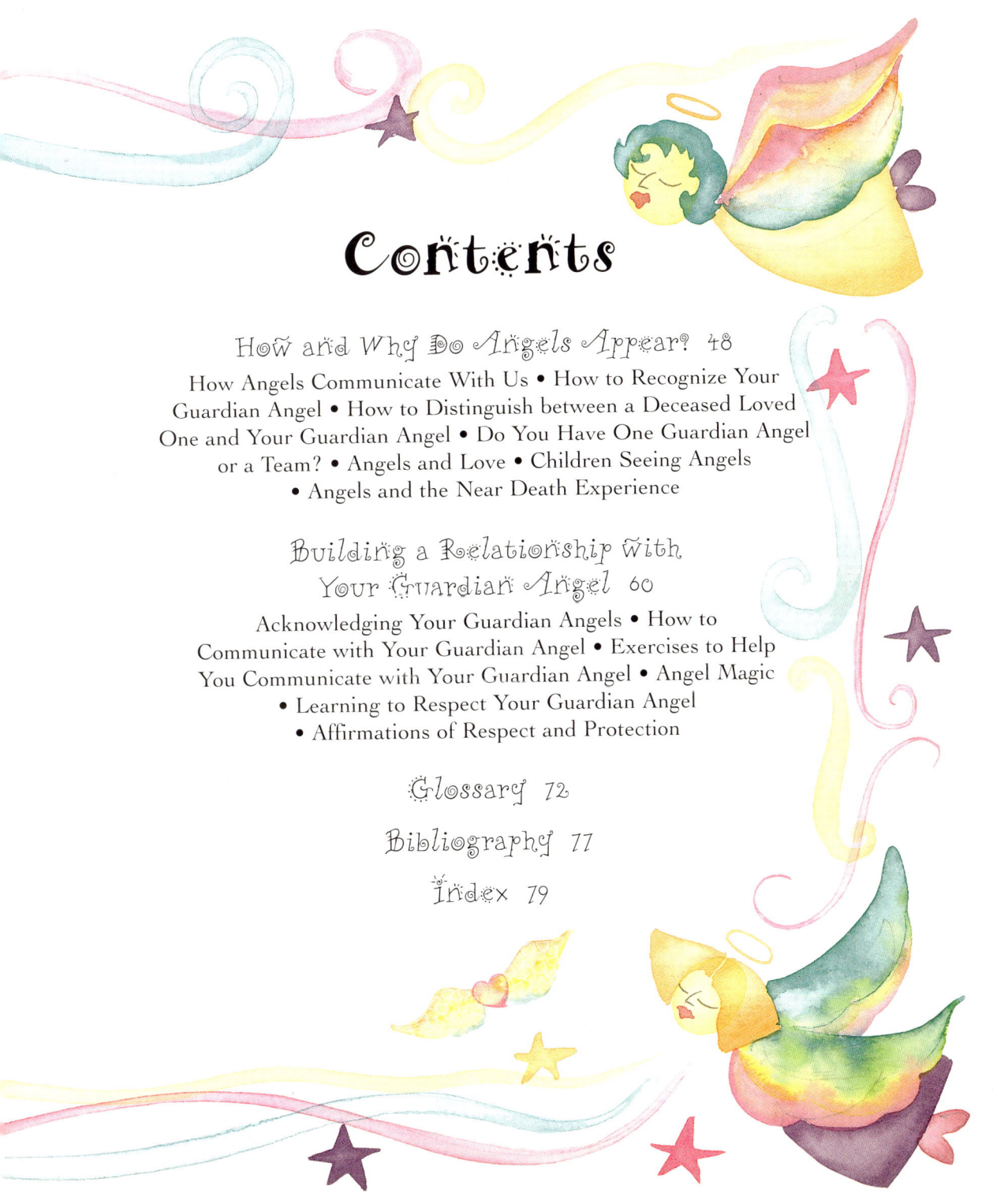

Contents

introduction

Images of babies with wings appeared in art works from the fourth century B.C. and on belts, buckles, mirrors, pendants and earrings made from precious metals and jewels. In this time of the new millennium, naked babies with wings are again appearing in great abundance on jewelry, notepaper, cards, t-shirts, and wherever the human imagination can put them. We know these little creatures as cherubs or cupids, and we associate them with all aspects of love and protection.

Invisible beings that act as messengers between heaven and earth, who guide, protect and advise humans, have been a significant part of every religious or spiritual belief system the world has known. These beings assume many forms and communicate in a variety of ways, always in a manner that will be recognizable to the culture or person that needs their help. While their differences from culture to culture are minor, you will see in the pages of this book that their similarities are profound, despite the distances in time and space. We in the West call them angels — they are also known as gods, spirits, ancestors, bodhisattvas, avatars, asparas, ghandarvas, devas and fairies. All these you will find in this book, as well as some of their evil counterparts. You will follow the fascinating evolution of the Western concept of angels from the ancient world through to modern times. This book will show you how angels have been portrayed in art and literature and how they have inspired many of the greatest artists and writers of all time. You will even be introduced to the ancient art of angel magic and the Hebrew mystical tradition of the Kabbala.

There are many orders of angels. Some keep the universe working as it should while others care for our world Angels who are concerned with the affairs of humankind are called, in Western religion, archangels The angels that are assigned to us at birth to look after our individual destinies are our guardian angels, and those that work at keeping our planet beautiful are the devas and nature spirits. This book is mainly concerned with these classes of angels and their equivalents in other cultures.

All societies have the concept of a guardian spirit or angel that is devoted to our spiritual and material well-being. Many cultures acknowledge their guardian spirits as part of their daily lives, while we in the West have been encouraged to let go of such notions and to regard them as childish, sentimental or superstitious. Most scientists believe that these angelic beings are no more than a culture's anthropomorphization of the forces of nature. That means that in order to make sense of the things that happen, a society or a person will attribute human characteristics to inanimate objects, such as plants and land forms, and to the elements. This way they create a pantheon of invisible beings. While there might be some truth in this theory, it is limiting to believe that this is the whole story. The fact that something cannot be perceived by one or more of the five senses, does not mean that it doesn't exist — science is full of technology that makes use of natural phenomena "not perceived" in previous eras.

Such thinking is not true of all scientists. Einstein stated: "I believe in God ... who reveals Himself in the orderly harmony of the universe. I believe that Intelligence is manifested throughout all Nature. The basis of scientific work is the conviction that the world is an ordered and comprehensible entity and not a thing of chance."

Perhaps the time has arrived when society's beliefs have come full circle. Advanced medical technology has enabled us to bring people back to life. In the section entitled ANGELS AND THE NEAR DEATH EXPERIENCE you will notice the irony that the strongest circumstantial evidence supporting the existence of life after death and the existence of angels has come from this technology. And no one can deny that the more technological and volatile our world gets, the more conscious our society becomes of spiritual concepts. For instance, countless people meditate every day to reduce stress — not too long ago, meditation was a purely spiritual practice.

We all have a guardian angel working to help us in our lives, trying to inspire us to achieve and encourage us through difficult times, but we very often ignore our angels simply because we don't know that they are trying to communicate with us. This is a great shame, for our lives would be greatly enriched if only we knew how to listen to them. Through this book you will discover how to recognize the presence of your guardian angel. You will also learn ways to connect with your guardian angel and consciously allow it to help you improve the quality of your life. And in the section on the devas and nature spirits, you will see how you can help these wonderful beings of light counter the effects caused by the misuse of technology.

Some mystics have proposed that angels are the thoughts of God. So, for those who wonder why we need angels when we have God, consider this: When you are connecting with an angel, you are connecting with the Supreme Being; after all, if someone connects with your thoughts, are they not connecting with you at a most profound level?

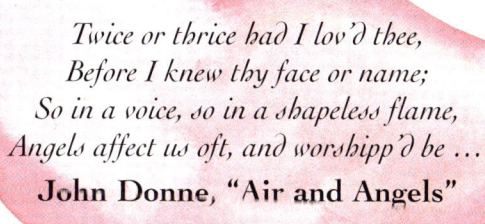

Twice or thrice had I lov'd thee,
Before I knew thy face or name;
So in a voice, so in a shapeless flame,
Angels affect us oft, and worshipp'd be ...

John Donne, "Air and Angels"

What is an Angel?

While there is a popular notion of angels sitting on clouds, playing harps with beatific expressions, they are in fact workers, just like humans. Their mission is to guide all living beings toward the Light of which they are a part.

To feel the presence of an angel is to know pure joy. Angels are all about us, desiring nothing more than to guide us toward what is good and protect us from that which will cause us harm. To benefit from their guidance, all you need are the ears to hear their words. They are there to help you when you are suffering grief, if you are willing to open yourself up to their healing presence.

The Presence of Angels

It is difficult for most people to believe in something that they cannot see, and few people have seen angels. However, if you will trust in yourself enough to open up your heart and your mind, you will, at the very least, be able to feel your angel's presence. You will see from this book that strange things happen in life that have no scientific explanation, but which are so "ordered" and of such a wonderful nature, that they cannot be considered random events.

Lives have been saved, life-altering mistakes have been avoided, and simple pleasures have been enjoyed. People who go on to share great loves meet by "the strangest coincidence" — "It was meant to be" is what most people say.

Angels and their labors shine with unearthly light, a light that is perceived at some level of consciousness by anyone who is open to receiving gladness in their lives. Throughout time, spirits and deities have been associated with light — the ancient Egyptians called their gods the "shining ones".

To learn more about the role angels play in our lives, read the chapter THE ROLE OF ANGELS, pages 40–47; and to enhance your life by engaging with your angel, read BUILDING A RELATIONSHIP WITH YOUR GUARDIAN ANGEL, pages 60–71.

Unless you can love, as the angels may,
With the breadth of heaven betwixt you;
Unless you can dream that his faith is fast,
Through behoving and unbehoving;
Unless you can die when the dream is past
Oh, never call it loving!

Robert Browning,
"A Woman's Shortcomings"

Visions of Angels

Their garments are white, but with an unearthly whiteness. I cannot describe it, because it cannot be compared to earthly whiteness; it is much softer to the eye. These bright Angels are enveloped in a light so different from ours that by comparison everything else seems dark. When you see a band of fifty, you are lost in amazement. They seem clothed with golden plates, constantly moving, like so many suns.

French curé, Père Lamy.

… the luminous quality gradually became normal in me, and at times in meditation there broke in on me an almost intolerable lustre of light, pure and shining faces, dazzling processions of figures, most ancient, ancient places and peoples, and landscapes lovely as the lost Eden.

Irish poet and mystic, Æ (George Russell), from *The Candle of Vision*.

Then there was an intensity of light before my eyes like the flashing of sunlight through a crystal. It widened like the opening of a gate and I saw the light was streaming from the heart of a glowing figure. Its body was pervaded with light as if sunfire rather than blood ran through its limbs. Light streams flowed from it. It moved over me along the winds, carrying a harp, and there was a circling of golden hair that swept across the strings. Birds flew about it, and over the brows was a fiery plumage as of wings of outspread flame. On the face was an ecstasy of beauty and immortal youth.

Æ (George Russell), from *The Candle of Vision*.

There are various layers of force within the auras of the angels, each layer with its own hues and direction of flow. The general effect is of brilliantly coloured ... flowing forces ... in constant, wavelike motion. Through these many auric emanations, from within outwards, streams of radiant energy, often white and of dazzling brightness, are continually flashing.

**Clairvoyant and mystic, Geoffrey Hodson, from
*Man's Supersensory and Spiritual Powers.***

The saintly multitude lay before my eyes like a snow-white rose, which Christ in his own blood had made his bride. Meanwhile, the angels, who soar aloft to gaze and celebrate the glory of him whom they love, hovered around. Like a troop of bees, now alighting, now clustering, their labors were fragrant and glowing. They flew downward to the mighty flower then rose from the petals, streaming upward to the endless dwelling of their joy. Their faces were of flame, their wings were of gold, and their dress was whiter than the purest snow.

Italian poet, Dante, from "Paradiso".

And Jacob went out from Be'er-she'ba, and went toward Ha'ran. And he lighted upon a certain place, and tarried there all night, because the sun was set; and he took of the stones of that place, and put them for his pillows, and lay down in that place to sleep.
And he dreamed, and behold a ladder set up on the earth, and the top of it reached heaven: and behold the angels of God ascending and descending on it. And behold, the Lord stood above it, and said, I am the Lord God of Abraham thy father, and the God of Isaac: the land whereon thou liest, to thy will I give it, and to thy seed.

Old Testament, Genesis 28:10–13

Angels Through Time

T he word "angel" comes from the Greek *angelos*, which is the equivalent of the Hebrew *mal'akh* meaning "messenger". The ancient Greek philosopher Socrates stated that: "God does not deal directly with man; it is by means of spirits that all the intercourse and communication of gods with men, both in waking life and in sleep, is carried on."

The Ancient World

Before angels, there were gods and goddesses, ancestors, and great spirit entities. These celestial beings, like angels, were charged to maintain harmony within the known universe; they were also messengers between heaven and earth. In the polytheistic religions of the ancient world, such as the religion of the ancient Greeks, the people worshipped a pantheon of male and female deities. The most important gods did not involve themselves with human daily life, while the least important were the most directly concerned. Rituals and sacrifices would be made to ensure the support of these deities, who could be benevolent or malevolent according to whim. The people held many festivals throughout the year to honor individual gods and goddesses, performed rituals and sacrifices, and prayed to them for intervention in their crises.

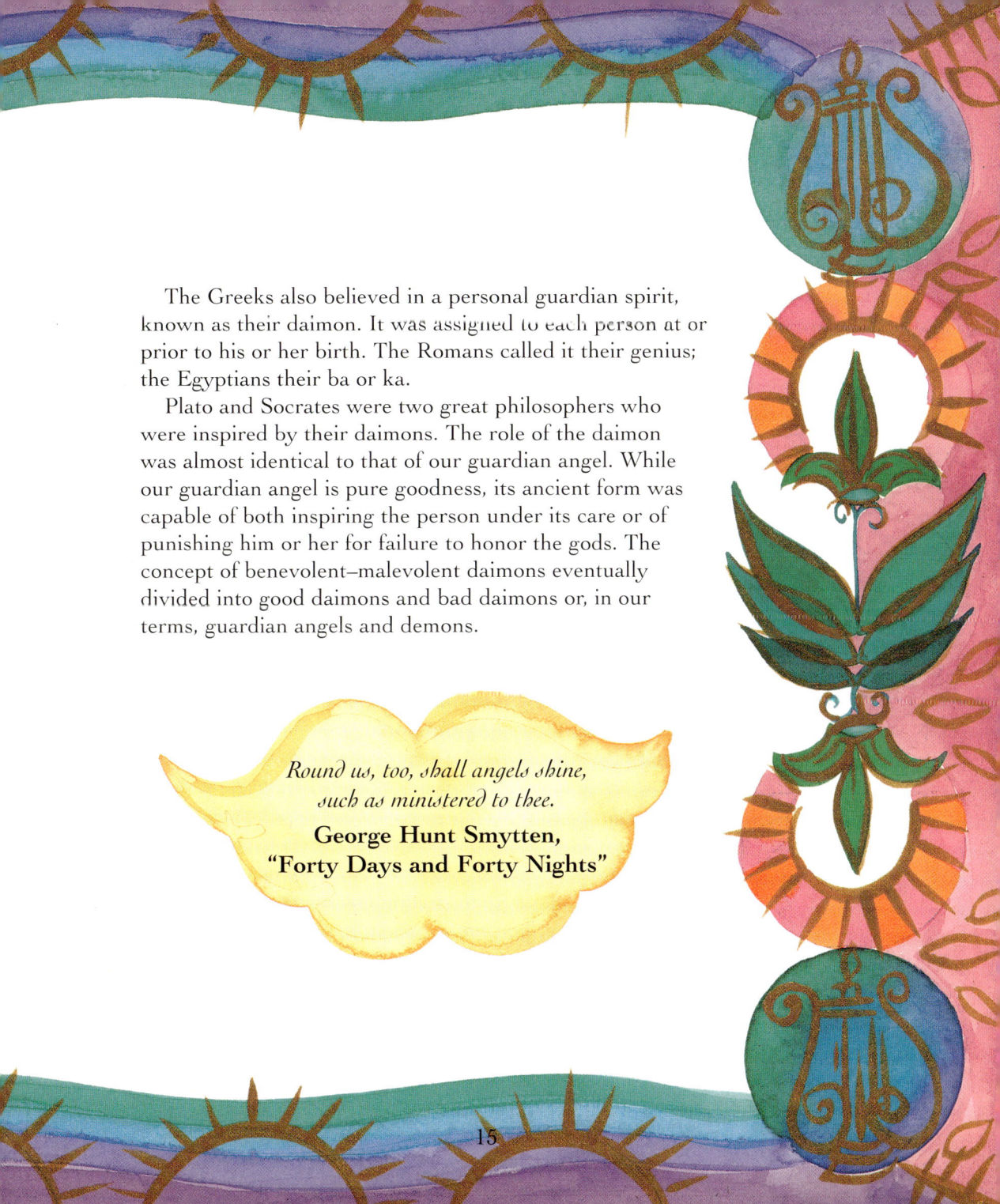

The Greeks also believed in a personal guardian spirit, known as their daimon. It was assigned to each person at or prior to his or her birth. The Romans called it their genius; the Egyptians their ba or ka.

Plato and Socrates were two great philosophers who were inspired by their daimons. The role of the daimon was almost identical to that of our guardian angel. While our guardian angel is pure goodness, its ancient form was capable of both inspiring the person under its care or of punishing him or her for failure to honor the gods. The concept of benevolent–malevolent daimons eventually divided into good daimons and bad daimons or, in our terms, guardian angels and demons.

Round us, too, shall angels shine,
such as ministered to thee.

George Hunt Smytten,
"Forty Days and Forty Nights"

The Beginning of Western Religion

Angels as we in the West understand them had their origins in the ancient Persian religion of Zoroastrianism. Zoroaster (c.628 B.C.– c.551 B.C.), also known as Zarathustra, came from a family of the lower nobility. He was a priest in the polytheistic religion of Persia, until he had a vision from Ahura Mazda, the Wise Lord. The vision showed Zoroaster that Ahura Mazda, as creator of heaven and earth, the source of light and darkness, the center of nature, the lawgiver, and the judge of the world, was alone worthy of worship.

Free will was an important concept of Zoroastrianism, not only for humans but for the gods as well. At the beginning of time, members of the pantheon had to decide whether they would follow Ahura Mazda or join Angra Mainyu (later Ahriman), the evil spirit of Zoroastrianism. Seven celestial beings known as amesha spentas or "beneficent immortals" supported Ahura in the great war against Angra Mainyu. Seven major gods joined Angra Mainyu.

Zoroaster preached that human beings were important soldiers in the war between heaven (Kingdom of Justice and Truth) and hell (Kingdom of the Lie). They, like the immortals, were given free will to choose to fight alongside the amesha spentas or join the evil forces. The amesha spentas were equivalent to our archangels, and the people would pray to them individually for intercession in their affairs. Humankind also venerated fravashis, who were similar in nature to the saints and whose aid could be sought in times of trouble. Every person was protected by a fravarti, which corresponds to our guardian angel.

Zoroaster was one of the most significant personalities in history. He was one of Pythagorus' teachers and was believed to have been a mystic, magician and occultist of great power. Zoroastrianism survived in Persia until the Arab-Islamic invasion of the seventh century. It still survives in India and Iran as Parsiism.

Some Zoroastrian Angels

Each of the Zoroastrian angels represents a facet of the divine nature of their father, Ahura Mazda or God. Humans were meant to share in the qualities personified by each one, hence their collective title "Beneficent Immortals".

Spenta Mainyu (Holy Spirit) is an aspect of God, created by him to fight Angra Mainyu. He also protects the sky, water, earth, plants, and unborn children.

Vohyu Manah (Righteous Thinking) is the firstborn son who sits at God's right hand. He is the personification of God's wisdom, illumination and love. It was he who guided Zoroaster to God's throne. He is the spirit of divine wisdom, illumination and love.

Asha Vahishta (Justice, Truth) is the most beautiful son of God. The believers pray that they may dwell with him in paradise. He protects the world from disease and evil. He presides over fire, sacred symbol of the divine and purifier of evil.

Khshathra Vairya (Desirable Dominion) presides over the kingdom of heaven, and on earth protects and gives strength to the poor, the sick and the weak. He presides over metal and the believer can realize the power of this element by allowing himself to be guided by this angel of Excellent Order and Good Mind.

Spenta Armaiti (Beneficent Devotion) is God's first daughter and sits at his left hand. She presides over Earth and guides and protects the believer. She is the spirit of devotion and faith.

Also participating in the battle between heaven and hell are the warrior band formed by all the guardian angels of humankind, the fravartis.

Judaism

In the Old Testament, angels acted as messengers of Yahweh, protected biblical personages, aided the prophets, and revealed God's word to humankind. They were the heavenly hosts that fought the powers of evil.

While there are seven archangels mentioned in the Old Testament, only four are named. They are: **Michael**, warrior leader of the heavenly army; **Gabriel**, the messenger; **Raphael**, God's helper; and **Uriel**, Light of God, the angel of prophecy and interpretation. There is some debate about the identity of the Old Testament's **Angel of the Lord**, sometimes referred to as "the Lord". It appeared as a disembodied voice, in human form dressed in animal skins, in visions, and it spoke to Moses from the burning bush about the plight of the people of Israel under Pharaoh. It has been speculated that this angel is Yahweh himself or Metatron, the angel closest to him, who was once Enoch. Many cultures hold the belief that God's light is so intense that no human being can behold it — in this case, intermediaries and messengers would be necessary, even for such a great prophet as Moses.

In other writings there are many more mentions of angels. Ten archangels are of particular importance in the Hebrew mystical tradition of the Kabbala (see next pages).

Judaism's Most Evil Angels

Samael, also known as Satan, is chief of the fallen angels and Angel of Death. He was one of the greatest angels, known as the Adversary, before his descent into hell. **Leviathan** is the monster of evil, a crooked serpent; he is the female sea-dragon, the hippopotamus, the crocodile, and the great whale. **Azazel** is the chief of the lower demons and teaches men to create weapons and women to tempt men. **Rahab** is the demon of chaos and the angel of insolence and pride. He attempted to stop the Hebrews from crossing the Red Sea. **Lilith** is Satan's bride. She was Adam's first wife and spends eternity trying to ensnare mankind.

Angels and the Kabbala

When God communicated the Torah to Moses, secret knowledge was believed to have been contained within the divine revelation. This knowledge, known as the Kabbala, was handed down, generation by generation. While it has undergone transformations over the centuries, its basic concept has remained constant. The Kabbala is Judaism's mystical tradition, highly complex and ritualistic, and one in which angels play important roles.

The icon of the Kabbala is known as the Tree of Life (for diagram see page 21). The Tree represents the ten stages of the universe both seen and unseen that was called into being by ten utterances of God, and is believed to be the model for everything that will ever come into existence. These ten stages are collectively known as the Sefirot, each representing one of the ten Divine Attributes. The Tree holds these Attributes in a fixed set of relationships that are governed by Divine principles. While the Tree is identified as Attributes of God, it is also representative of human experience, as we are created in the image of God.

The Divine principles are expressed in the three pillars of the Tree of Life — the Left, the Right and the Middle. They govern the relationships between the Sefirot, thus achieving perfect balance. The Left pillar is the side of power, justice and constraint. It represents the fearsome awe of God and if unrestrained, evil will rise. The Right pillar represents expansion, mercy, unity, harmony and benevolence. The Middle pillar represents equilibrium and grace, the ideal balance between Divine mercy and justice. The angel closest to God, Metatron, communicates grace to his twin brother, the angel of Earth Sandalphon, down the Middle pillar, and humankind may climb it to reach spiritual perfection.

Each Sefira is governed by an angel. See page 20 to discover who they are. In addition, the Kabbalists say that both an angel and a demon hover around each person while he or she makes moral choices.

It is a Jewish belief that at the beginning of every day God creates a legion of angels who sing before him then disappear — they continue to be formed with every breath God takes.

19

The Ten Holy Sefirot and Their Governing Angels

Sefira	Archangel	
KETER Divine Crown	Metatron	The angel closest to God, he is the link between the Divine and humankind. He was Enoch before his physical ascension to heaven. Chief of the hayyoth hakodesh ("holy beasts"). Metatron was counselor to Moses.
HOKHMAH Wisdom	Raziel	Wisdom personified and the Angel of Mysteries. Chief of the arelim ("the valiant ones"). Raziel was Adam's counselor.
BINAH Understanding	Zaphkiel	Angel of Contemplation.
HESED Mercy	Zadkiel	Chief of the order of hashmallim or dominions. He is the Angel of Benevolence, the Angel of Mercy and the Angel of Justice. Zadkiel was Abraham's counselor.
DIN Justice, Might, Judgment, Power	Samael	The adversary who represents the severity of God. A chief of the seraphim and leader of 12,000 angels of destruction. Also Angel of Death.
TIF`ERET Beauty, Glory	Michael	The sun in splendor, chief of the heavenly hosts, Angel of the Presence, Angel of Repentance, Angel of Righteousness, Angel of Mercy and Angel of Sanctification. Michael was counselor to Solomon.
NEZAH Endurance, Victory, Eternity	Haniel	"He who sees God" and chief of the tarshishim ("brilliant ones"). Haniel transported Enoch to heaven.
HOD Majesty, Splendor	Raphael	The Angel of Healing both of the world and humankind, Angel of Compassion and Love. Chief of bene elim, the host of angels who unceasingly sing the praises of God. Raphael was counselor to Isaac.
YESOD Foundation	Gabriel	The prince of justice and chief of the ophanim or kerubim (wheels or chariots). He is the Angel of Mercy, Angel of Vengeance, Angel of Death and Angel of Revelation. Gabriel was counselor to Joshua and Daniel.
SHEKHINAH God's Presence in the World, Kingdom	Sandalphon	Twin brother of Metatron and originally the prophet Elias. He is the tallest angel, his feet are on Earth while his head reaches heaven. He ensures the prayers of the faithful ascend as an orb to God. Sandalphon is the Guardian Angel of Earth and is involved in ceaseless combat with Samael.

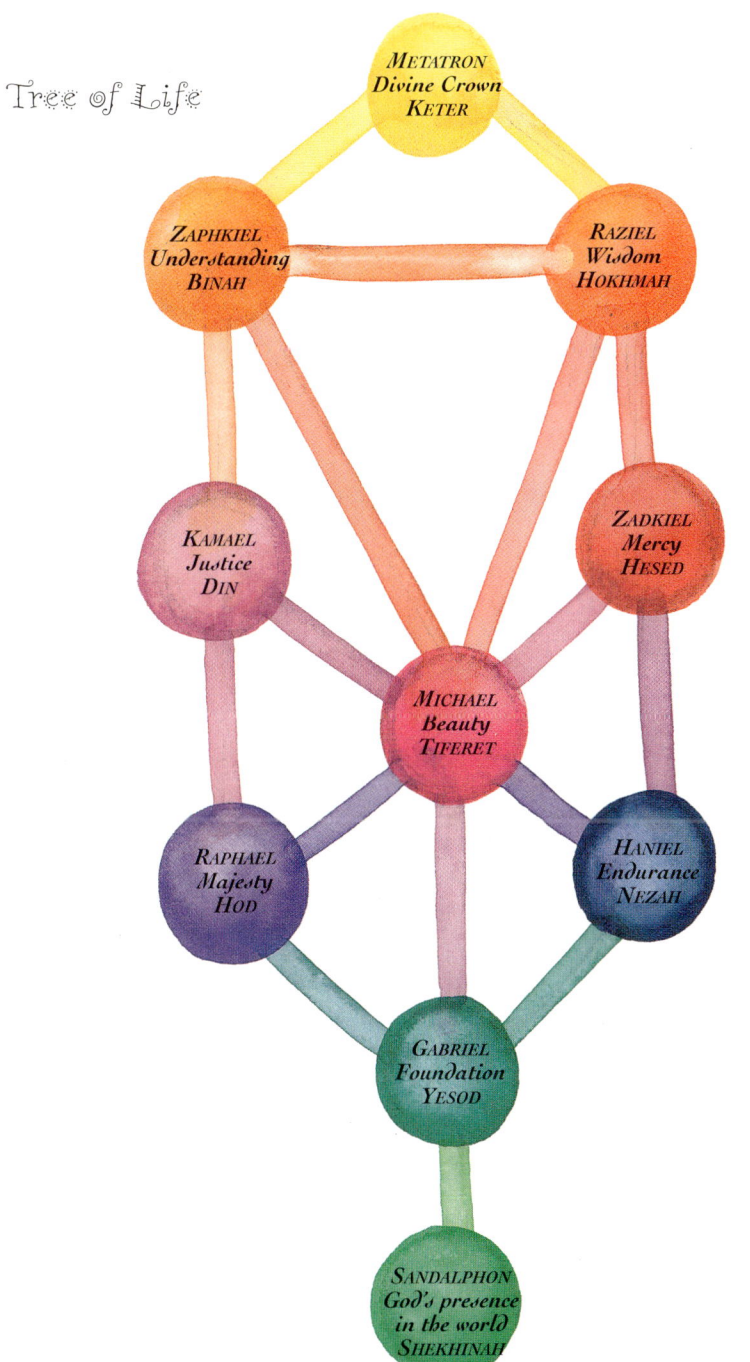

Tree of Life

METATRON
Divine Crown
KETER

ZAPHKIEL
Understanding
BINAH

RAZIEL
Wisdom
HOKHMAH

KAMAEL
Justice
DIN

ZADKIEL
Mercy
HESED

MICHAEL
Beauty
TIFERET

RAPHAEL
Majesty
HOD

HANIEL
Endurance
NEZAH

GABRIEL
Foundation
YESOD

SANDALPHON
God's presence
in the world
SHEKHINAH

Christianity

Christianity embraced angels like no religion before it. However, the love of angels came from the people rather than the Church fathers. In the letter of Paul to the Colossians, St. Paul is contemptuous of the adoration of angels. He wrote: "Let no one disqualify you, insisting on self-abasement and worship of angels, taking his stand on visions, puffed up without reason by his sensuous mind, and not holding fast to the Head …" This suggests that even at this early time there were many who were having "visions" of angels. Perhaps what Paul witnessed was something like the angel mania of the Middle Ages.

During this period there was a great acceptance of the idea of "visions", especially in England and France. Monks and nuns were so obsessed by angels that they would have countless visions of angels appearing to them and giving them advice. Some of these episodes were likely to have been the result of hysteria, caused by fervent praying and self-flagellation, fuelled by the desperate desire to see angels.

In this time of the new millennium in the Christian countries of the West, people are again becoming more conscious of angels, though without the hysteria of the Middle Ages. Essential to the traditional Christian concept of angels are the hierarchy of the Nine Celestial Orders of Angels and the story of the Annunciation.

The concept of angels has widened to include a simple, secular belief. While a Catholic will pray to an archangel for spiritual guidance and ask for help from his or her guardian angel, many people "see" angels or "feel" their presence in nature, in their homes, in their places of work.

The Nine Celestial Orders of Angels

Seraphim are the highest order of angels. They are the guardians before God's throne. They are referred to as the "burning ones" because they are aflame with love for God. God's grace flows through the seraphim to the angels below, dispelling darkness and purifying the universe. They call one to another: "Holy, holy, holy is the Lord of hosts; the whole earth is full of his glory."

Cherubim are God's record keepers and guardians of God's glory. The Lord God placed the cherubim at the east of the garden of Eden to guard the way to the tree of life. They are the charioteers of God and bearers of his throne.

Thrones consider how God's decisions should be manifested and bring about justice according to universal laws.

Dominions decide what needs to be done to accomplish God's needs, and regulate the duties of angels to ensure the universe keeps working as it should. Through them the majesty of God is manifested.

Virtues draw on God's force to work miracles on earth. They bestow grace and valor on the worthy.

Powers keep order in the universe and the demons from overthrowing the world.

Principalities keep watch over nations and attempt to inspire their leaders to make wise decisions. They are also protectors of religion.

Archangels look after the affairs of humankind, as they relate to God's will, and to act as messengers and intermediaries between God and the human race. They act as guardian angels to leaders of world movements.

Angels include guardian angels, who are assigned by God to every human being at the time of his or her birth. Angels of this order are assigned to assist every aspect of life in the universe.

The Story of the Birth of Christ — the Annunciation

The angel Gabriel was sent by God into Nazareth, a city of Galilee, to a virgin named Mary who was engaged to a man named Joseph who belonged to the House of David. Gabriel appeared before the virgin and said: "Hail, though that art highly favored, the Lord is with thee. Blessed art though among women."

Mary was troubled by this and wondered what kind of salutation this was. Then the angel Gabriel said: "Fear not, Mary, for thou hast found favor with God. Though shalt conceive in thy womb, and bring forth a son, and shalt call his name Jesus. He shall be great, and shall be called the Son of the Highest, and the Lord God shall give unto him the throne of his father David. And he shall reign over the house of Jacob forever; and of his kingdom there shall be no end."

Then Mary said to the angel: "How shall this be, seeing I have never been with a man?"

And the angel said: "The Holy Ghost shall come upon thee, and the power of the Highest shall overshadow thee. Therefore that holy thing which shall be born of thee shall be called the Son of God."

And Mary said: "I am the handmaiden of the Lord. Let it be as you say."

Mary was not yet Joseph's wife, and it became known that she was with child. An angel of the Lord appeared to Joseph in a dream, saying: "Joseph, fear not to take Mary as thy wife, for that which is conceived within her is of the Holy Ghost, and though shalt call him Jesus for he shall save his people from their sins."

When a decree went out from Caesar Augustus that all the world would be taxed, everyone went into his own city. And Joseph went up from Galilee into Judea to Bethlehem. Mary was heavy with child and soon she delivered her firstborn son. She wrapped him in swaddling clothes and laid him in a manger, because there was no room for them in the inn.

Meanwhile, shepherds were in the field, keeping watch over their flock by night. And the angel of the Lord came upon them, and the glory of the Lord shone around them, and they were afraid. The angel Gabriel said: "Fear not, for I bring you good tidings of great joy, which shall come to all the people. Unto you is born this day in the city of David a Savior, which is Christ the Lord. And this shall be a sign to you: You shall find the babe wrapped in swaddling clothes, lying in a manger."

Suddenly, there was with the angel a multitude of the heavenly host praising God, singing: "Glory to God in the highest, and on earth peace, good will toward men."

When the angels ascended into heaven, the shepherds said one to another: "Let us now go to Bethlehem, and see this that the Lord has made known to us." And they came with haste, and found Mary, Joseph, and the babe lying in a manger.

Three wise men from the East saw the star that told them the King of the Jews had been born. They followed the star which went before them until it came and hovered over where the young child was. And they saw the child with Mary his mother, and fell down and worshipped him, and presented him with their gifts of gold, frankincense and myrrh.

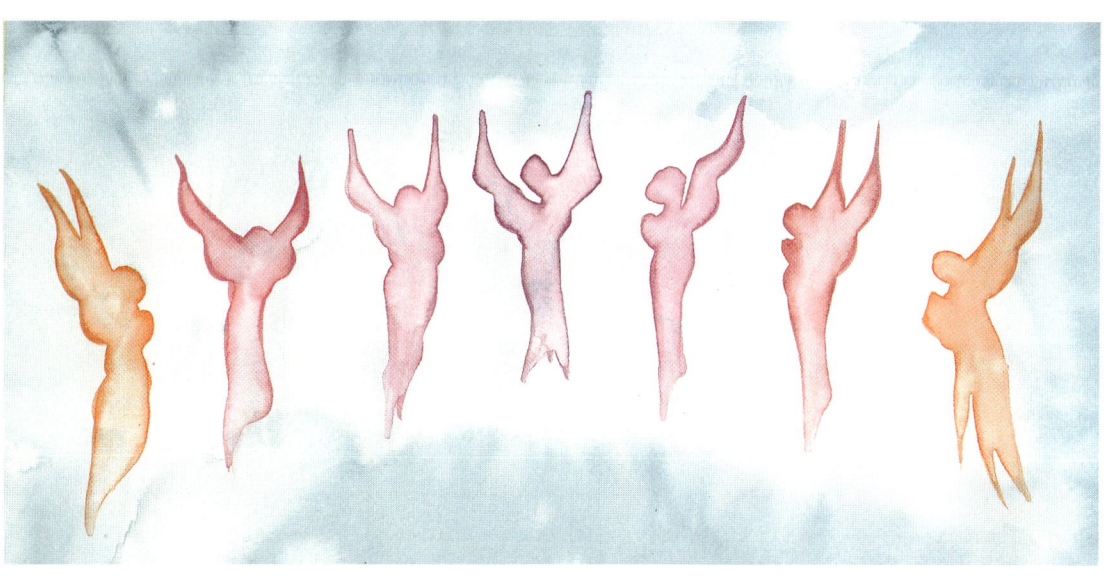

The Archangels

The best known angels are the archangels Michael, Gabriel, Raphael and Uriel. They have featured in many great art works and have played significant roles in religious history. The three lesser known archangels are Haniel, Raguel and Barakiel.

Michael was the first angel created by God. He is the ruling prince of the seraphim, and it was he who threw Satan out of Heaven after the war in Heaven. Michael was the angel who spoke to Moses on Mount Sinai.

Gabriel is the messenger. He appeared to the Virgin Mary to announce that she would be the mother of Christ and appeared to Zachariah to announce the birth of John the Baptist. He is the ruling prince of the cherubim.

Raphael is the angel of the spirits of humankind and thus the supervisor of guardian angels. He is also the healer and the guardian of young people. It is Raphael's job to heal the earth that has been defiled by Satan and his helpers, and it was he who warned Adam about the dangers of sin. He is the ruling prince of the virtues.

Uriel is the angel of Light and the angel who wielded the fiery sword as he drove Adam and Eve from the Garden of Eden. He is the angel of prophecy and warned Noah about the Flood. He also predicted the coming of the Jewish Messiah.

Haniel is the "glory or grace of God". He is invoked as a guardian against evil. He is the ruling prince of the principalities.

Raguel is an angel of earth. He brings erring angels to account, punishing them accordingly.

Barakiel is known as "lightning of God". He is invoked to bring success in games of chance.

Guardian Angels

There are references throughout the Bible to guardian angels and, as such, they are part of Church doctrine. Origen, the third-century Christian mystic and theologian, said that guardian angels, the invisible protector assigned by God to each of us at birth to guide us in good thoughts, words and deeds, were around all Christians and could be treated as "kinsfolk and friends … who make their presence felt intimately to those who pray to them."

Belief in guardian angels was especially strong in the fourth century. The great men of that time were in open and constant conversation with their guardian angels. They would ask for inspiration, protection and aid in times of crisis, and credit their guardian angels for leading them to the right people at the right time, and for inspiration and well-made decisions — Constantine prepared himself for his conquests with visions of his guardian angel.

In the Roman Catholic Church calendar October 2 is the day for honoring guardian angels.

A Note on the Fallen Angels

Writings of the Western religions include stories telling of angels falling from grace. At the basis of these religions is the perpetual war between the powers of Light and those of the Dark. Every soul that does evil strengthens the side of the Dark and each soul that acts with selflessness and courage brings Light to the world. While the purpose of angels is to help individuals and the whole of humankind toward the Light of God, the purpose of demons and devils is to put temptation — traditionally of a material or sexual nature — in the way of these journeys.

The archdemon is known by several names in the Christian faith: Satan, Christ's enemy; Lucifer, the fallen Light Bearer; and Beelzebub, the Lord of the Flies (or the Lord of Dung). Originally, Archdemon Satan was once a great angel, a leader of the seraphim.

Islam

The angels of Islam are glorious. Their celestial might is captured in imagery that is rich and full of color and passion. Allah created Israfil. Five thousand years later, Allah created Mika'il. Five hundred years after that, he created Jibra'il. These, along with Azrael, the Angel of Death, are the four main angels of Islam. But there are literally millions of angels according to Islam, because Mohammed said that every manifestation of creation, even a single raindrop, is accompanied by an angel.

Israfil is "the burning one". The feet of this most powerful of the angels are under the earth while his head reaches to the pillars of the Divine Throne. He is covered from the soles of his feet to the top of his head with hairs and with tongues that glorify Allah in a thousand languages. And from his breath, Allah creates a million angels who glorify Him. Israfil is the angel of music and is the most beautiful being in Creation. His compassion is so great that he looks down into Hell three times each day and three times each night, whereupon he weeps tears for the agony he sees there. If Allah did not continually stop his tears, the world would soon be flooded. It is Israfil who will blow the trumpet on Judgment Day. On the third and final blast the world will be consumed by fire.

Mika'il is Michael. He lives "on the borders of the Full Sea, crowded with an innumerable array of angels". His wings are of green the color of emeralds. He is covered from the top of his head to his feet with hairs of saffron. Each hair bears a million faces and each face a million eyes and a million tongues. Seventy thousand tears for the sins of the faithful fall from each eye, and the tongues, in a million languages, beg forgiveness from Allah.

Jibra'il is Gabriel, the Angel of Truth. It was he who dictated the Koran to Mohammed. His hair is of saffron and is of the brightness of the moon and stars. He enters the Ocean of Light 360 times each day, and when he emerges, from each of his 1,600 wings a million drops fall to become angels who sing the praises of Allah. The sun is between his eyes as are the words: "There is no god but God, and Mohammed is the Prophet of God".

Azrael is the Angel of Death. He is immense, vaster than all the heavens, and he turns the world between his hands. He has four faces and 4,000 wings. His body is covered with as many eyes and tongues as there are human beings on the earth. All of God's creatures are shielded from his image by a million veils.

Malik is a righteous angel and guard of djahannam, the Muslim hell. He is assisted by 19 angels known as zabaniya. This is a place of boiling water and pus where infidels are roasted and the souls of Muslim sinners are seared by the fires and tormented by Malik. While the infidels suffer for eternity without mercy, the faithful are there for a time only and may escape the torture by repeatedly crying out: "Allah, the Compassionate, the Merciful."

Islam's Guardian Angels

The guardian angels of Islam are known as the hafaza. Each person has four: two to watch over him or her during the day and two at night. They protect the person against evil jinn (demons) and write down every good thing and bad that the person does; this information is to be used as evidence on Judgment Day.

Hinduism

Brahma, Vishnu and Shiva are aspects of the
Supreme Lord, who is beyond existence.
Vishnu incarnates periodically to destroy
the evil in the world. His incarnations
on earth are known as avatars, the
most important being Krishna.

Between the infinite and the world of
matter is the domain of the devas or gods, which
are close in nature to the archangels, and the ghandharvas and
asparas, which are equivalent to the angels. The ghandharvas are
musicians and male; the asparas are dancers and female. Male and
female, melody and rhythm, together they create the harmony of the
universe. Ghandarvas hear the Divine Song and channel it through to
the world. And a mystic can experience the ecstasy of paradise through a
symbolic marriage to an aspara.

Buddhism

Bodhisattvas are the Buddhist's equivalent to our angels. People ask for
their help in all matters of life. Bodhisattvas can be in either human or
celestial form. Many great teachers are considered to be bodhisattvas,
and anyone may work toward attaining this step before Buddhahood.

The word bodhisattva is a Sanskrit word meaning: "whose being or
essence is enlightenment". The bodhisattva represents compassion; he has
achieved perfection, yet of his own free will chooses to participate in the
sorrows of the world. Some are even believed to reside in hell to aid and
comfort those who suffer there.

The most powerful and most loved bodhisattva of Mahayana Buddhism
is the Lotus Bearer, Avalokiteshvara. He reveals himself in human form
with two arms, or in the form of a deity with four, six, twelve, or a
thousand arms, and in one of his left hands he holds the lotus of the world.

In China and Japan Avalokiteshvara is also represented as the female
Kwan Yin of China or Kwannon of Japan.

Animism and the Role of the Shaman

When a society believes that spirits inhabit trees, rocks, mountains, rivers and the cosmos, it is called an animist society. Animism is believed to be the original religion of humankind. It still exists in many tribal societies, and there are a growing number of ordinary people in Western societies who are returning to the belief that spirits do indeed dwell within all things — these spirits are referred to as nature spirits, fairies, devas and angels. See page 47 for the story of the Findhorn Garden Community where these beliefs were acted upon and a miracle occurred.

In tribal groups, the shaman intercedes for his village to the spirits for their aid in healing the sick, aiding the hunt, or ensuring a good crop. Ritual is essential when the shaman wishes to communicate to the supernatural world; it not only denotes the greatest respect, but reflects the proper order of things. The spirits will meet with the shaman when he dreams or is in a trance to instruct and counsel. Often during ritual, the shaman will ingest an hallucinogenic plant, such as peyote or datura, and embark on a "flight" into the spirit world.

The role of guardian angel falls to the ancestors in many tribal societies and in China and Japan. The ancestors are venerated and rituals are performed to ensure their continued support in the person's health, happiness and good fortune.

To see the importance of ritual in communicating with your guardian angel and how to use it, see chapter BUILDING A RELATIONSHIP WITH YOUR GUARDIAN ANGEL, pages 60–71.

Angels in the Arts

Angels have played a significant role in the creative life of humankind from the beginning of time. An aeon ago, the shaman would begin a ritual of chanting, singing and dancing, while beating bones together to create rhythmic vibrations. He would then go into a trance state and in his spirit form would visit with the gods, the spirits or the ancestors. These inhabitants of the other world would tell the shaman stories about themselves or about matters which would affect the tribe. When the shaman returned to his body, he would relate these stories to his village in vivid detail. Music and storytelling were essential means of communication with the spirit entities that cared for and guarded the tribe.

The Inspiration of Angels

The ancient Greeks believed that their daimon — their guardian angel — inspired their poetry, art and philosophy. The Old Testament shows that the function of angels was to reveal to humankind the stories of God and the angels and how the world came into being. The Koran was dictated to Mohammed by the archangel Gabriel. Indeed, religious tradition across the globe states that angels created language itself.

In the first millennium in Europe, the illiterate would contemplate stone carvings in churches and cathedrals to learn the stories of the great events and figures of the Bible. The thirteenth century saw vividly colored images of sky, doves, tendrils, vegetation and flowers, and of angels bearing crosses flying from heaven toward earth. By the time of the Renaissance, angels were featured in most religious art. Michaelangelo, the great Renaissance sculptor and painter, believed that within every block of marble was an angel waiting to be released. Angels appeared in many shapes and sizes, and were clearly beloved of all the painters. One of the favorite themes of the painters of this period was the Annunciation (see pages 24–25).

And yet, as angels in some brighter dreams
Call to the soul when man doth sleep,
So some strange thoughts transcend our wonted
themes, And into glory peep.

Henry Vaughan,
"They Are All Gone"

What Angel is That?

When you look at the great religious paintings of the Renaissance, you will notice many strange creatures. These are depictions of the greatest of the Nine Celestial Orders of Angels that were inspired by descriptions in the Bible and by those provided by a sixth-century Middle Eastern writer known as Pseudo-Dionysis in his Celestial Hierarchies. See below for clues on how to identify just what angel you are looking at.

Seraphim are "the burning ones" and are colored a flaming red and/or gold to symbolize fire. A seraph has three pairs of wings. Two of its wings cover its face, two cover its feet and the other two are outstretched, for with these it flies.

Cherubim have undergone radical transformations in their representations over 3,000 years from the Assyrian leonine-monster guardian to the winged creature of the Old Testament (see WHAT EZEKIEL SAW on pages 36–37) to a chubby baby with blue wings (see CHERUBS AND CUPIDS opposite). In early Christian art the cherubim were usually depicted with human heads that were often round and chubby, and with blue wings covering their bodies. Sometimes they were depicted as having whole human bodies with blue wings. In Renaissance art their transformation to the fat babies with blue wings began. The blue color symbolized the sky.

Thrones were portrayed as winged wheels within wheels, whose rims were covered in eyes (see WHAT EZEKIEL SAW on pages 36–37). The next three orders are shown as humanlike.

Dominions have two wings, may be crowned and carry a seal with a monogram of Jesus in the right hand and in the left a staff surmounted by a cross.

Virtues hold lilies or red roses and, like the powers, are depicted in long, golden robes with green stoles. These orders hold gold staves in their right hand and a seal of God in the left.

Principalities and **archangels** are portrayed in soldier's garb and sandals.

Angels are usually seen in plain white gowns and are barefoot.

Cherubs and Cupids

The most beloved of all the angels is the pudgy, rosy-cheeked, naked baby with wings, known as the cherub or cupid. It made its first appearance in the art works of the fourth century B.C. This was Cupid, son of Venus, goddess of love, and Mercury, the winged messenger to the gods. Cupid was usually portrayed with a quiver of arrows and a bow, often in the act of piercing the heart of a mortal with the flame of love.

From the fourteenth century in Italy, a similar figure began appearing in religious artworks. Here he is an angel known as a cherub. He has blue wings and hovers above the Madonna and Child or plays musical instruments to entertain them; he also attends to the child Christ. The image as we know it today was crystallized by the sixteenth-century painter Raphael. He merged the identities of the Christian cherub and the pagan Cupid, and together it became known as *putto*.

The cherub as baby is a long way from its original incarnation as the Assyrian guardian monster of 3,000 years ago. Then the cherub appears in the Old Testament with four faces and four wings (see story WHAT EZEKIEL SAW, page 36). As for Cupid, in an earlier time in ancient Greece, he was a beautiful youth named Eros, the god of love.

The gradual change from winged monster with the leonine face to cute baby has been the subject of speculation and scholarship for medievalists and theologians for a long time. The two images seem to be a universe apart, but are they? The more modern version embodies innocence, spiritual purity and unconditional love; it also has the ear of God. In this way, this naked baby with the blue wings has as much power and more as that of its Assyrian progenitor.

What Ezekiel Saw

This is a retelling of the vision experienced by the Old Testament prophet Ezekiel that was a favorite subject for Renaissance religious painters. The four creatures are the cherubim and the wheels are the angels known as the order of thrones.

In the land of the Chaldeans, when I, Ezekiel the priest, son of Buzi, was captive by the River Chebar, the word of the Lord came to me. This is how it happened. From the north came a whirlwind and with it a great cloud. The cloud was surrounded by brightness and within it a fire was unfolding. From out of the fire came four living creatures.

They had the likeness of a man, but every one had four faces and four wings, and they sparkled like burnished brass. Their feet were straight, but with soles like that of a calf's foot. They had the hands of a man under the wings on each of their four sides. Two wings of each one covered its body. The other two wings were stretched out, joining one creature to another. They moved straight forward, without turning as they went. As for their four faces, they each had the face of a man on one side, the face of a lion on the right side, the face of an ox on the left, and the face of an eagle on the other. Something like that of burning coals went up and down among the creatures, and out of the fire came flashes of lightning.

As I looked upon the creatures, beside each one I saw one wheel upon the earth. The wheels were the color of golden green chrysolite and their appearance was of a wheel within a wheel. The rims of the wheels were full of eyes, and everywhere the four creatures went, the wheels went with them. When the creatures were lifted up from the earth, the wheels were lifted with them, for within each of the wheels was a living spirit.

Spread above the heads of these creatures was something like the vault of heaven, shining like a terrible crystal. And when the creatures rose I heard the noise of their wings, which was like the thunder of great waters and the voice of the Almighty and the noise of a multitude. Then, when they were still, they let down their wings.

Above that which shone like crystal over their heads was the likeness of a throne, its color and luster that of sapphire. And upon this throne was the likeness of a human form, gleaming with the appearance of fire, and all about him was a brightness, such as that of a rainbow. Here was the likeness of the glory of the Lord, and I fell upon my face before it.

Some of the Great Angel Painters

Fra Angelico (c.1400–1455) is considered to be the supreme angel artist. Michaelangelo was said to have exclaimed: "Angelico must have seen these angels in heaven, otherwise he could never have painted them as he has done." This is quite possible, since Fra Angelico belonged to the monastic order of Dominicans, an order which required a great deal of spiritual contemplation. Legend has it that Fra Angelico would see his room filled with angels during his morning meditation.

Botticelli (1445–1510) calculated that the world would end in 1503. In his famous painting *The Mystic Nativity* about the Adoration of Mary of the shepherds at the birth of Christ, angels and humans embrace and tiny demons are staked to the ground.

Raphael (1483–1520) was particularly fond of the putti or baby cherubs, the final incarnation of the mighty cherubim of the Old Testament. A fine example of *putti* are in his painting *The Triumph of Galatea.*

William Blake (1757–1827) claimed that his paintings were fragments of his visions. His angels are represented as beings of swift movement and of light, unlike the solid figures of previous times.

Gustav Doré (1832–1883) is famous for his illustrations of Dante's *The Divine Comedy* and Milton's *Paradise Lost*. Angels glow in their multitudes in his detailed illustrations of black and white.

Two Literary Masterpieces

The Italian **Dante Aligheri** (1265–1321) and **John Milton** (1608–1674), an English Puritan, are the authors of the two most loved literary works about angels. Dante wrote a trilogy based on his visions of hell (Inferno), purgatory (Purgatorio) and heaven (Paradiso) called *The Divine Comedy*. Dante is taken on a tour of hell and purgatory by the Roman poet Virgil, and into paradise by his beloved Beatrice who died young. The descriptions of demons and angels are extraordinary.

Milton's *Paradise Lost* is about the war of might in heaven, when Lucifer rebels against God, is thrown out of heaven and his subsequent corruption of Adam and Eve. *Paradise Lost* is regarded as the greatest epic poem in the English language.

Angels in Popular Culture

Guardian angels entered the popular arena with the 1946 film, *It's a Wonderful Life*. James Stewart plays a character named George Bailey who, facing bankruptcy, wants to end his meaningless, failed life. Clarence, George's guardian angel, materializes to stop George from jumping off a bridge. When George declares that he wished he'd never been born, Clarence takes George through the life of his town as it would have been had George never been born. This shows George how his caring interventions prevented misery and catastrophe for the other people in the town. When George returns home after this encounter, he finds that the people of the town have collected all the money he needs to save himself from the financial ruin he was facing. Clarence leaves a note saying: "No man is a failure who has friends."

Since *It's a Wonderful Life* there have been many films and television series about guardian angels. *Highway to Heaven* and *Touched by an Angel* are examples of popular television shows about the intervention of guardian angels in the lives of ordinary people in crisis. In both cases, the guardian angel helps the individual get him or herself out of trouble and onto a new level of spiritual awareness. As time goes on, more and more films on this subject are produced and always with great success.

There are numerous book titles on the subject of angels or guardian angels in fiction and non-fiction, and it is interesting to note that angels are once again finding their way into works of literary fiction after a long period of intellectual contempt for such subjects. The arts reflect the society in which they were created. In this time of social and spiritual uncertainty, many people find the notion that angels are keeping watch over us gives them a sense of comfort and well-being.

39

The Role of Angels

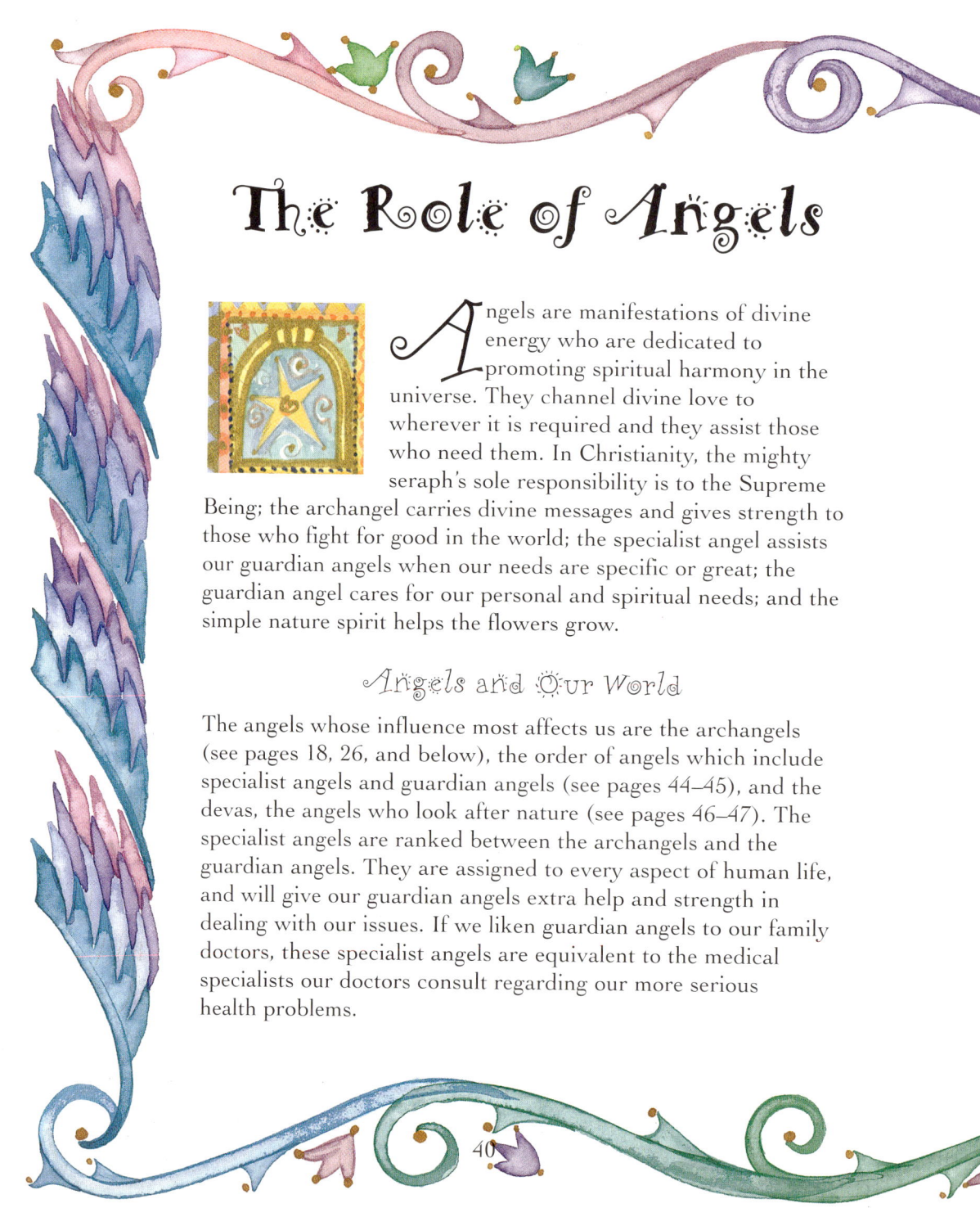

Angels are manifestations of divine energy who are dedicated to promoting spiritual harmony in the universe. They channel divine love to wherever it is required and they assist those who need them. In Christianity, the mighty seraph's sole responsibility is to the Supreme Being; the archangel carries divine messages and gives strength to those who fight for good in the world; the specialist angel assists our guardian angels when our needs are specific or great; the guardian angel cares for our personal and spiritual needs; and the simple nature spirit helps the flowers grow.

Angels and Our World

The angels whose influence most affects us are the archangels (see pages 18, 26, and below), the order of angels which include specialist angels and guardian angels (see pages 44–45), and the devas, the angels who look after nature (see pages 46–47). The specialist angels are ranked between the archangels and the guardian angels. They are assigned to every aspect of human life, and will give our guardian angels extra help and strength in dealing with our issues. If we liken guardian angels to our family doctors, these specialist angels are equivalent to the medical specialists our doctors consult regarding our more serious health problems.

National leaders have the power to destroy humanity and the globe. Their work is so demanding and critical that the order of principalities (see page 23) are assigned to them. Archangels are guardian angels to the leaders of major movements that try to make the world a better place. Their mission is to inspire these leaders, advise them and give them courage, usually through the mediums of intuition and dream (see next chapter HOW AND WHY ANGELS APPEAR). No matter how powerful these angels may be, they do not have the authority to force leaders to act wisely; all they can do is try to influence their decisions.

The story on the next two pages is about a great leader who altered the course of history by following the guidance of the archangel Michael and two martyred saints.

Angels descending, bringing from above,
Echoes of mercy, whispers of love.
Fanny J. Crosby,
"Blessed Assurance"

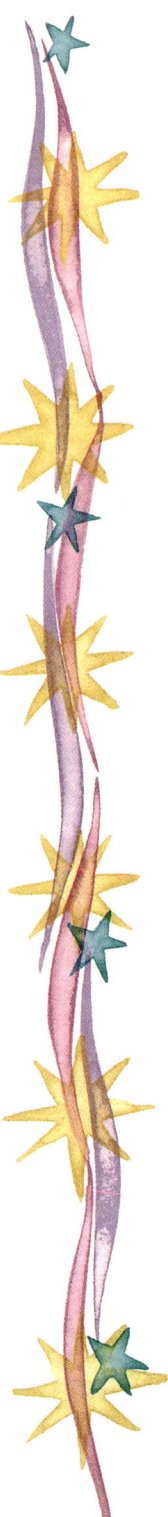

The Story of Joan of Arc

Joan of Arc was born a peasant in 1412. From a very early age, Joan had been hearing the voices of the archangel Michael and St. Margaret of Antioch and St. Catherine of Alexandria. It was these three who guided Joan in her short and extraordinary life during the Hundred Years War between France and England.

In 1429, under the guidance of her voices and dressed in men's clothes, Joan went to see the Dauphin of France. Charles had heard about her visions and disguised himself as one of his own courtiers, but Joan went straight to him. She told him of her mission and said that she would have him crowned king, a seemingly impossible ambition given his war with the Duke of Burgundy. When interrogated by Church authorities she said that she would give proof of her mission at Orléans, a city which had been under siege by the English for months.

Joan carried a standard carrying the image of Christ in Judgment and a banner bearing the name of Jesus. She declared that she would find her sword in the church of Saint-Catherine-de-Fierbois, and she did. On May 7 she and another commander attacked the English. All other commanders followed her example and the English retreated. She then promised the French complete victory over the English. The prediction proved correct as did another — carrying her banner, Joan stood near Charles VII during his coronation on July 17, 1429.

In May 1430 she was captured by the forces of the Duke of Burgundy. Because Charles was negotiating a truce with the Duke, he made no attempt to save her. For a fee of 10,000 francs, the Duke of Burgundy turned her over to the Bishop of Beauvais, an agent of the English. She was to be tried for heresy. The charges were that she followed the commands of her "voices" before those of the Church; that she claimed her pronouncements were made with divine authority; that she predicted the future; that she endorsed her letters with the names of Jesus and Mary; that she professed to be assured of salvation; and that she wore men's clothing.

Her interrogations began January 13, 1431 in the city of Rouen. She was chained to a wooden block and put in irons. When she fell ill, her persecutors threatened her with torture if she would not renounce her claims. When she refused, they turned her over to the secular authorities to be condemned to death.

She was taken to the cemetery of the church of Saint-Ouen where her sentence was read out. Full of terror, Joan agreed to all Church terms. She signed a confession, saying that this was "pleasing to our Lord." She was then returned to prison. She had been ordered to wear women's dress and at first she had obeyed. But soon she was again wearing men's clothing. She told the authorities that St. Catherine and St. Margaret were upset by her "treason" when she capitulated.

On May 30, 1431, Joan received Communion and, accompanied by two Dominicans, was taken to the Place du Vieux-Marché. A huge crowd had gathered to hear her sentence and watch her being led to the stake. The pyre was lit. Joan asked one of the Dominicans to hold the crucifix so she could see it and to call out the assurances of salvation so loudly that she would hear him above the flames. News of her execution was formally published by the English king and the University of Paris a few days later. She was nineteen years old.

Joan of Arc was canonized in 1920.

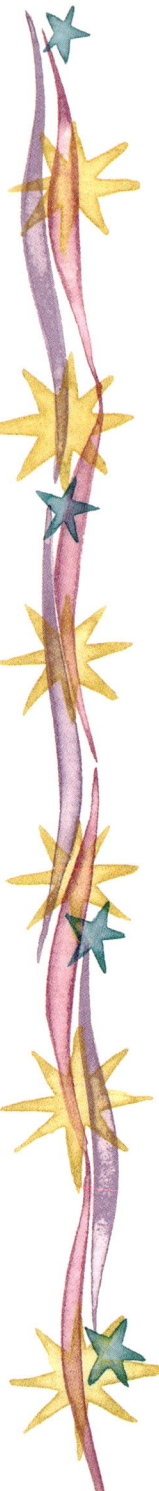

Guardian Angels

We all have the guidance, support, assistance and protection of a guardian angel to call upon in times of emotional confusion or in our quest for spiritual evolvement or when we are in danger. The personality of the guardian angel who is assigned to us is carefully chosen so that it complements our own personality. The reason why some people refer to a particular experience with guardian angels as "divine intervention" is usually because of the dramatic impact the experience has made on their lives.

If you can recall the number of times in your life when you were prompted to act purely on instinct, discarding logic, and when the result of such action was life enhancing, you might believe that a guardian angel was influencing your actions. Guardian angels seem to take particular care of us when we are traveling. Stories, such as the woman who falls asleep at the wheel of a car on a busy road and is woken sharply by a voice in her ear that warns of danger, are told so frequently that they could almost be called commonplace. Weary travelers who cannot explain how they made the final stages of a long journey without incident have been known to attribute their safe arrival to the intervention of an angel. It is important to note, however, that your guardian angel can warn you, most frequently by a strong intuitive feeling on your part, but they cannot force you to listen.

There are special affirmations which people use before setting out on a journey. They can be short and simple, such as:

*"Guardian angel who takes good care of me, protect me
from danger from the beginning to the end of my journey."*

Or you may wish to create a verse of your own which you commit to memory and recite daily, for example:

*"Whenever and wherever I may travel on this day,
I need my guardian angel to protect me all the way.
Place a circle of protective white light all around me,
With respect and hope I place my trust in you. So mote it be."*

Not all the work of guardian angels is so serious. You can ask them to help you find lost possessions or ensure that the traffic lights turn green for you when you are in a hurry. Of course, they won't always comply; they will judge the situation and decide if such help is warranted — after all, if everyone's guardian angels turned the lights green whenever their people wanted, there'd be utter chaos on the roads!

Guardian angels are highly evolved spirits who understand that while you are living on a material planet, you will need to learn material values as much as spiritual ones. They are here to help you balance the material with the spiritual. They respect the fact that you have a free will to make important decisions and choices, and though they may tug at your conscience when you flirt with danger, they understand that you must learn through experience. Guardian angels have no desire to intrude upon your privacy. It is not the role of your guardian angel to judge your lifestyle or beliefs.

Artists and Their Guardian Angels

From the time of the ancient Greeks, there have been many creative people who claim their inspiration comes from their daimon (see pages 15 and 32) or guardian angel. Some have believed that the angels are working through them, but this is highly unlikely. While it is true that all genuine creative people work from their intuition, the role of the guardian angel, the daimon or the muse, is only to help keep the creative channels open and the communication between the artist's unconscious and conscious flowing — angels are there to assist the creative process when asked, not to use people for their own ends.

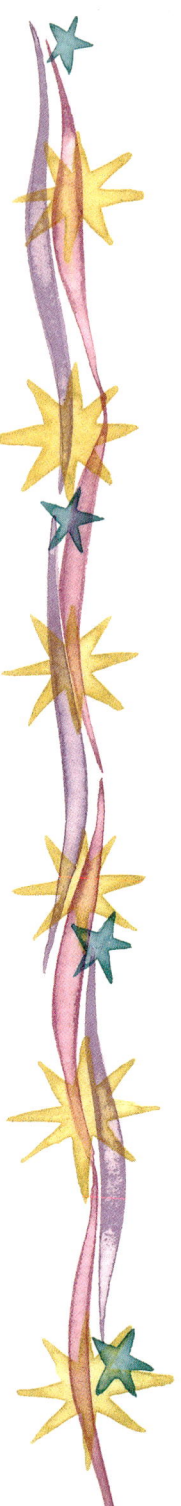

Devas, Fairies and Nature Spirits —
Guardian Angels to the Plants

Just as people have guardian angels, so too do all living things. Tribal groups have always recognized that plants, trees, animals and land forms have guardian spirits. There are hierarchies of spirits who care for nature. The highest order is the devas. The word is Sanskrit meaning "shining ones" and they are perhaps equivalent to the order of angels. Then there are the elementals or nature spirits of several classes, including fairies, elves and sprites.

Some people can see nature spirits, especially people from remote areas of Ireland and England — the Celtic world has never forgotten its fairies, big and small. Sometimes they appear as storybook fairies with gossamer wings, at other times they are perceived as flashes of light. Fairies, just like angels, will appear to you as you expect to see them.

However, it is not necessary to see nature spirits to benefit from their existence. There is a big difference between the gardens of those with "green thumbs" and those without. People without green thumbs can't understand why they don't get the same results, despite the fertilizers or the money they might spend on their gardens. By loving and honoring your plants, you will help the nature spirits in their work to make your plants strong and beautiful. Follow the example of the people of the Findhorn Community (see opposite) and your garden will be your own special paradise.

The Garden of Findhorn

The garden of Findhorn lies on the peninsula of Moray Firth in the north of Scotland on the North Sea approximately 600 miles (970 kilometers) south of the Arctic Circle. It is famous for the 40-pound cabbages and eight-foot delphiniums it once produced and the roses that grew in the snow, despite the battering the area received from icy winds.

It began in 1962, when three adults and two young boys decided to build a garden in the sand and gravel, among the spinifex and gorse. They arrived with a belief that they had something important to do there and lived with the principle that they had to surrender themselves entirely to God. They meditated and received guidance every day. With backbreaking work, they built up the soil with compost materials that came to them by "good fortune". They felt love for everything they did, and were aware of a sense of light passing through them into the ground.

The devas initiated communication with them, and told them that the garden was being created as an experiment of cooperation between the devic, the elemental and the human kingdoms. Peter Caddy was the human representative; his wife Eileen received messages from the God within her; Dorothy Maclean communicated with the devas and angels; and "Roc", a quiet scholarly man who joined the experiment in 1966, communicated with Pan and the elementals or nature spirits.

The devas told them that their thoughts and states of mind affected the garden; that the most important things they could do was to send positive radiation into the soil while cultivating it and to love the plants while tending them. This way they would be sensitive to the spiritual and material needs of the plants in their garden.

The extraordinary conditions of the early Findhorn garden came to a close by the early 1970s, but the garden and the community, now expanded to around three hundred members, are still there and flourishing.

How and Why Do Angels Appear

ngels are beings of light and the energy of love. Normally they are invisible to our eyes, but on rare occasions they will manifest themselves to us. The particular form a guardian angel chooses to present itself in will depend largely on the person's expectation of its appearance. The most common perception of a guardian angel's appearance is of a humanlike entity with flowing white robes and wings. In earlier times those wings would have been seen as feathered, but nowadays, wings of light would perhaps be the more common perception.

How Angels Communicate With Us

There have been reports of people who, during a dramatic escape from death by accident, have glimpsed a being of light intervening in the situation. However, the most common means guardian angels use to communicate with us is by using our own intuition, appearing to us in dreams or, occasionally, by sending a strong voice inside our heads. If you are now wondering how to tell the difference between an angel voice and the voices people with mental illnesses hear, it is important to realize that when an angel speaks to you inside your head, it is always good and loving, takes place only during an emergency or serious situation, and is very rare indeed. A person would be lucky to have one such incident in his or her life.

Angels will make their presence known to us, in one form or another, whenever we need them to. They are our guides and will use whatever means are necessary to get through to us, to offer us advice and comfort. The only person who can stop them from succeeding is you — your disbelief when they do appear will all but negate the fact that they have appeared.

Four angels to my bed,
Four angels round my head,
One to watch, and one to pray,
And two to bear my soul away.

Thomas Ady,
"A Candle in the Dark"

How to Recognize Your Guardian Angel

The loving energy emitted by a guardian angel is palpable to those who are open to receiving it and is one of the most powerful signs of their existence in our lives. It will create a feeling of protectiveness in times of fear or danger, and a calming reassurance in times of self-doubt.

When an Angel Appears in Your Dreams

The most documented method of guardian angels communicating to their people is through dream. Religious writings, including the Bible, and myth is full of accounts of angel communication using the medium of dream. There are certain signs that identify the person you are speaking with (or listening to) as your guardian angel if it appears to you in a dream. First, your guardian angel will always take the form of someone for whom you have the highest respect and you will feel surrounded by love, even if you are suffering extreme anguish. This could be a person you know, alive or dead; or it could take an archetypal form, such as an old man or woman. Some people with strong religious feelings could even see a priest or a nun. Your guardian angel will never appear to you in the form of a person or thing, either known to you or not, for which you have little or no respect.

The second indication that this entity is your guardian angel is that it will speak to you with great kindness. The voice will be clear and the message one of simple wisdom that will show you how to extricate yourself from the problem or sadness that you are experiencing. While we often dream that we are talking to people, we are not usually "hearing" words as such. Hearing someone speak clear words to you is extremely rare in dreams, and when it happens you must take notice of it.

To find out how to make yourself more open to receiving your guardian angel through the medium of dreaming, practice the exercise described on page 63.

50

When an Angel Speaks to You through Your Intuition

Everyone has intuition, but it is very difficult these days to hear it, let alone trust it, when our technological world is telling us that there is no such thing or that what we think of as intuition is really just our imagination working overtime.

In early times, and in the world of nature, intuition can mean the difference between life and death. For us, listening to our intuition will mean the difference between a life lived on the surface and one that is multi-dimensional.

Before you can trust your intuition, and therefore hear your angel speaking to you, you will need to be able to distinguish it from your fears or desires. The trouble is, that when we have an emotional investment in a situation or expect great things from it, we tend to stack the evidence in our own favor. The following gives you some idea of how to recognize the difference.

★ When your intuition is at work, or when your angel is speaking to you through it, you are conscious of receiving some information that you know to be true. There is a sense of peace or quiet about this knowledge. You can look at it as something that originated from outside yourself. This may cause you distress for the situation or great joy, but there is a sense of quiet behind whatever other emotions you may experience as a result of the message — in fact, your response would be similar to that on learning something important, and which you know to be true, from another individual. When you have an angel encounter, you will be left with a feeling of calm and that everything will be all right.

★ If your certainty about an issue is a result of your own hopes and fears, rather than your angel's advice, a sense of desperation may be underlying your joyfulness. A feeling of desperation will never accompany an angel encounter.

How to Distinguish between a Deceased Loved One and Your Guardian Angel

Some people become confused about the difference between encounters with guardian angels and deceased loved ones.

Very few people ever actually see their guardian angels whereas almost everyone sees a deceased loved one, either in dream or during that time between sleep and being awake. The sad part is that few people believe that they have had an encounter with their loved one, believing the vision to be a case of wishful thinking. A desire on the part of a deceased loved one to comfort and reassure his or her grieving family is the main reason they appear to us. They also want to convey to you that they are now supremely happy and not suffering in any way. The inner peace and happiness which the deceased loved one generates is sometimes so intense and unforgettable that it leaves the grieving person with the same degree of comfort and protection as that provided by a guardian angel. This leads to the belief that the deceased loved one has now become this person's new guardian angel.

There is no harm in being comforted by this line of thinking, nor would your guardian angel be offended by this confusion; after all, the role of a guardian angel includes its ability to understand all your emotions and everything that affects you. And for those who do recognize the encounter, grief usually ends, because these people know their loved one is still around and that they will be reunited some day.

Caution

Sometimes when a person can't accept the death of a loved one, he or she could be tempted to go to extraordinary lengths to make a communication happen. Playing with Ouija boards is one dangerous way that people use to contact the deceased. The biggest danger is that rarely does the dead relative communicate through these means. There are plenty of spirits out there who are unscrupulous at best and potentially very dangerous. Your guardian angel can only protect you if you do not willingly go into such a situation.

Do You Have One Guardian Angel or a Team?

If your life is pretty straightforward, there is usually no need for more than one guardian angel to look after you, but there are many people who feel very strongly that they have a team of guardian angels rather than just one. These people are usually very busy with lots of responsibility, and it is no doubt true that they do indeed have a team of angels looking after them.

For those of us who only have one guardian angel, there are times in our lives when our guardian angel requires help on our behalf. It might be during an illness suffered by you or a member of your family; there could be a crisis that has to be dealt with; or difficult enterprises that need to be undertaken. During these times try to have faith that your guardian angel has a grip on the situation and is bringing in whatever help is needed. Sometimes that help will come from specialist angels, such as healing angels, or from the guardian angels of other people connected to the situation.

World leaders

Certainly world leaders have a team of guardian angels who would work under the guidance of an archangel. It is unfortunate that so many people in power will close themselves off from this help — it is also fortunate for the world that many leaders listen, at least unconsciously, to their guardian angels. Many well-known psychics have claimed to see the guardian angel of such leaders standing or hovering around them during public appearances.

People Who Work for the Good of Others

Anyone who works for the welfare of a number of people will have a team of guardian angels who will draw on help from specialist angels. Spiritual healers and medical practitioners work with a team of angels, their own and those of their patients, together with specialist healing angels. School teachers often receive help from the children's guardian angels.

Angels and Love

Of all the karmic lessons with which our guardian angels try to help us, the greatest is love, because love is what binds us together and gives us insight and wisdom. Matters of the heart will challenge every emotion and fulfill or destroy our hopes, dreams and wishes. Without love in our lives, our souls are impoverished. When we experience love, we are optimistic, energetic and happy — we also feel motivated to share our good feelings with others.

Guardian angels try to show us that we are worthy of being loved and that we should never settle for less than the real thing. But we are free to make our own choices, even when those choices lead to disaster. Love of self, love of a partner, love of family and friends, and especially love of children, can all bring rewards, but also sadness or regret. Our guardian angels understand those times when we are confused by the difficult decisions with which love can confront us, and so they try to guide our actions.

Our guardian angels cannot choose a partner for us, but they will help us find our true soul mates, sometimes performing little miracles to do so. All aspects of love are great and provide opportunities to learn generosity of spirit and the joy of receiving love. We learn valuable lessons in tolerance and patience and we learn how to share.

Many people think that when a personal relationship fails, the whole experience was a waste of time and effort. Here guardian angels can be of great benefit to you. Nothing you do or experience is wasted. If you suffer pain, there is something you can learn from it. Listen to your intuition and note your dreams. Your guardian angel is sure to be showing you what it is you need to gain from the experience. Understand the lesson and you will not repeat it in your next relationship.

How Your Angel Can Help You Find Your Soul Mate

Every one has a soul mate, but he or she might not be there for you right now. Be happy being with yourself for the moment and take the time to release any negative attitudes you might have toward love relationships. Love baths are a powerful way of merging body and soul and opening your psychic centers. This will enhance contact with your guardian angel, as well as making you aware of your soul mate when you meet him or her. Have your love bath immediately before going to bed, every night if possible, as this will encourage conscious communication with your guardian angel. Choose some romantic music, a beautiful candle and two or three essential oils from the box below.

Love bath

Run a warm bath and sprinkle 3 drops of each of your chosen essential oils, swishing water to thoroughly disperse the oils. Place your candle where you can watch the flame flickering, and light it. While you soak in the warm water, be conscious of how the water feels against your skin. Breathe in the scents and with half-closed eyes watch the flame of the candle. Try to visualize your guardian angel and feel love toward it. Allow yourself to receive the love of your guardian angel. Soak in the love that is flowing between you and your angel and feel the warm water caressing your body. Expand those loving feelings outward into the world, while asking your guardian angel to direct your love and generosity to the person who is your soul mate.

Take note of your dreams for signs of your soul mate, and note what your intuition tells you on first meeting a possible partner. The more you practice this exercise and the others in this book, the more open you will be to receiving pure love and meeting your soul mate.

Essential Oils for Your Love Bath

Sensual	*Evocative*
Clary Sage	Bergamot
Ginger	Cedarwood
Jasmine	Frankincense
Neroli	Geranium
Patchouli	Lavender
Rose	Lime
Sandalwood	Orange
Ylang-ylang	Rosewood

Children Seeing Angels

Perhaps the reason some children see angels is because they are closer to the world of the angels than the one they have more recently entered, and so they remember how to communicate with them.

Believing and trusting in guardian angels can create a wonderful sense of protectiveness and personal well-being in children. They love to talk about and communicate with their guardian angels, and many even draw pictures of them. Some also like to exchange angel stories and, unless they are dissuaded to do so, they like to be able to share their experiences with their parents.

Exercises to help your child have beautiful dreams

There are some simple and enjoyable exercises which children can do to enhance their guardian angel encounters, like the one below.

Encourage the child to create a little verse which they can easily commit to memory and which they can recite every night before going to sleep.

"Sweet dreams by guardian angel
Stay with me throughout the night
Stand by my side and share my dreams
Until the morning light."

Tell the child to close his or her eyes and picture a rainbow stretching from his or her room into a dreamland where only good people and good things happen. Tell your child to imagine that this is a magic rainbow which he or she can travel along with his or her guardian angel into this beautiful place where they can play and laugh and talk with the angels. Here they can also sleep with the angels until morning, when they will travel back along the rainbow and the child can wake up in his or her own bed, feeling happy and relaxed.

Another exercise you can do with your child is to suggest that he or she imagines seeing a bright star surrounded by golden light, and that this star can lead him or her toward a dreamland where, protected by a guardian angel, magic and miracles can happen without harm or discomfort.

Children who practice exercises like this usually report wonderful dreams which they can later write about and draw pictures of the images they have seen.

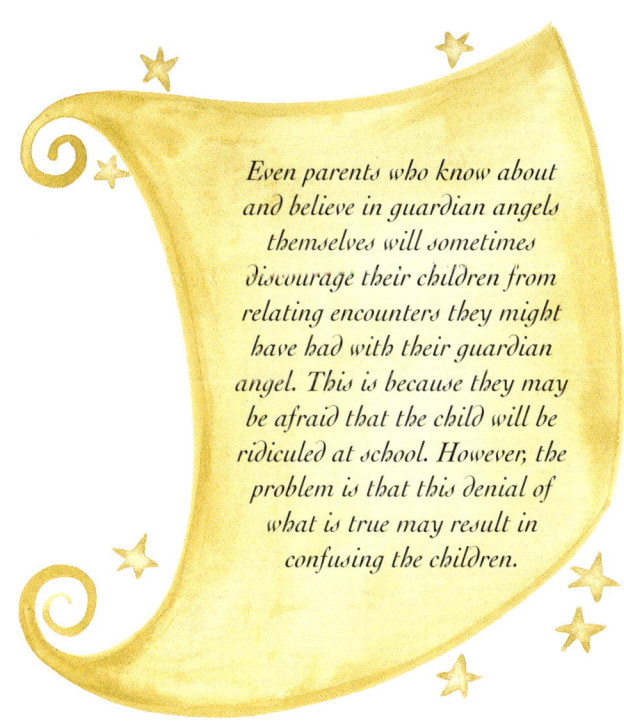

Even parents who know about and believe in guardian angels themselves will sometimes discourage their children from relating encounters they might have had with their guardian angel. This is because they may be afraid that the child will be ridiculed at school. However, the problem is that this denial of what is true may result in confusing the children.

Angels and the Near Death Experience

Since Raymond Moody, Jr. M.D. published his book *Life After Life* in 1975 reports of people remembering their experiences during the time they were pronounced clinically dead are becoming almost commonplace. Dr. Moody called this phenomenon the "near-death experience". While no two near-death experiences are identical, they all have elements in common. Some people will experience all facets of the experience, while others may only experience one or two. The length of time a person is "dead" will often determine the depth of his or her experience.

For those whose experience goes beyond the first stages of hearing noises, such as buzzing, whirring or bells, and floating out of the body, the most profound elements involve contact with spiritual beings, some seen and some sensed, which surround the person with acceptance, love and serenity. These entities are often identified by the person as spirit guides to help him or her in his or her transition. Sometimes they are deceased loved ones but often they are figures that were previously unknown to the person. In rare cases, this figure will identify itself as the person's guardian spirit.

The most profound element of the near-death experience is the being of light at the other end of the dark tunnel. Only those who are "dead" for a longer period of time will experience full contact with this being. The light is extremely bright, yet does not hurt the eyes. It makes the person feel extremely loved and serene and conveys conversation to the person through thought, while showing him or her a panoramic display of his or her life. People who have experienced this being of light say that it is impossible to misinterpret what it is saying to you and extremely difficult to relate in human language what was said, though all agree that it is not judgmental and its concern is that you love fully and learn the lessons of life. While the experience of this being does not vary from individual to individual, its identity does. It has been identified as Jesus or Christ, Mary, Mohammed, an angel, and other spiritual figures significant to the beliefs of the person concerned or, when the person has no prior spiritual beliefs, it is identified simply as "the being of light".

People who experience this phenomenon are always transformed by it. Their attitude to life changes for the better; they are no longer afraid of death, many even looking forward to it, but they love life more and desire to contribute to the well-being of others. Many people without religious beliefs who come back from this experience become very spiritual and sometimes religious.

There is considerable research being done on this phenomenon by medical doctors and others. Apart from those who have actually experienced it, health care workers are primary sources of this research, for they are there to hear patients' stories upon resuscitation. They are also the caregivers of dying patients. They listen to patients speak of "seeing" angels hovering about them in the days and weeks prior to their deaths and, in the final hours, will observe them speaking with unseen identities, usually identified as deceased relatives and friends. Children in particular speak of angels.

While skeptics will say that these experiences are induced by dreams, hallucinations, oxygen deprivation, chemicals from the brain, or drugs, research has shown that these alternatives do not satisfactorily explain the phenomenon of the near-death experience.

Building a Relationship with Your Guardian Angel

Building a relationship with your guardian angel is no more difficult and certainly no less rewarding than the effort you would put into building a friendship with anyone else you love and respect. Acknowledgment, trust, respect and loyalty are the key words which should guide you in your quest to achieve a compatible and lasting bond with your guardian angel. It is essential that you understand the importance of these qualities when you set out to achieve what is in effect priceless.

Acknowledging your Guardian Angel

The following are guidelines that will help you in your quest.

★ A simple greeting as you begin each day and a thank you as you bid goodnight will be appreciated as acknowledgment of your guardian angel's presence.

★ If you feel inclined, wear an angel pendant or pin as a statement of your belief and faith in guardian angels.

★ Pledge your trust each day by chanting a short silent affirmation. For example:

"Guardian angel, in whom I trust, guide my actions today."

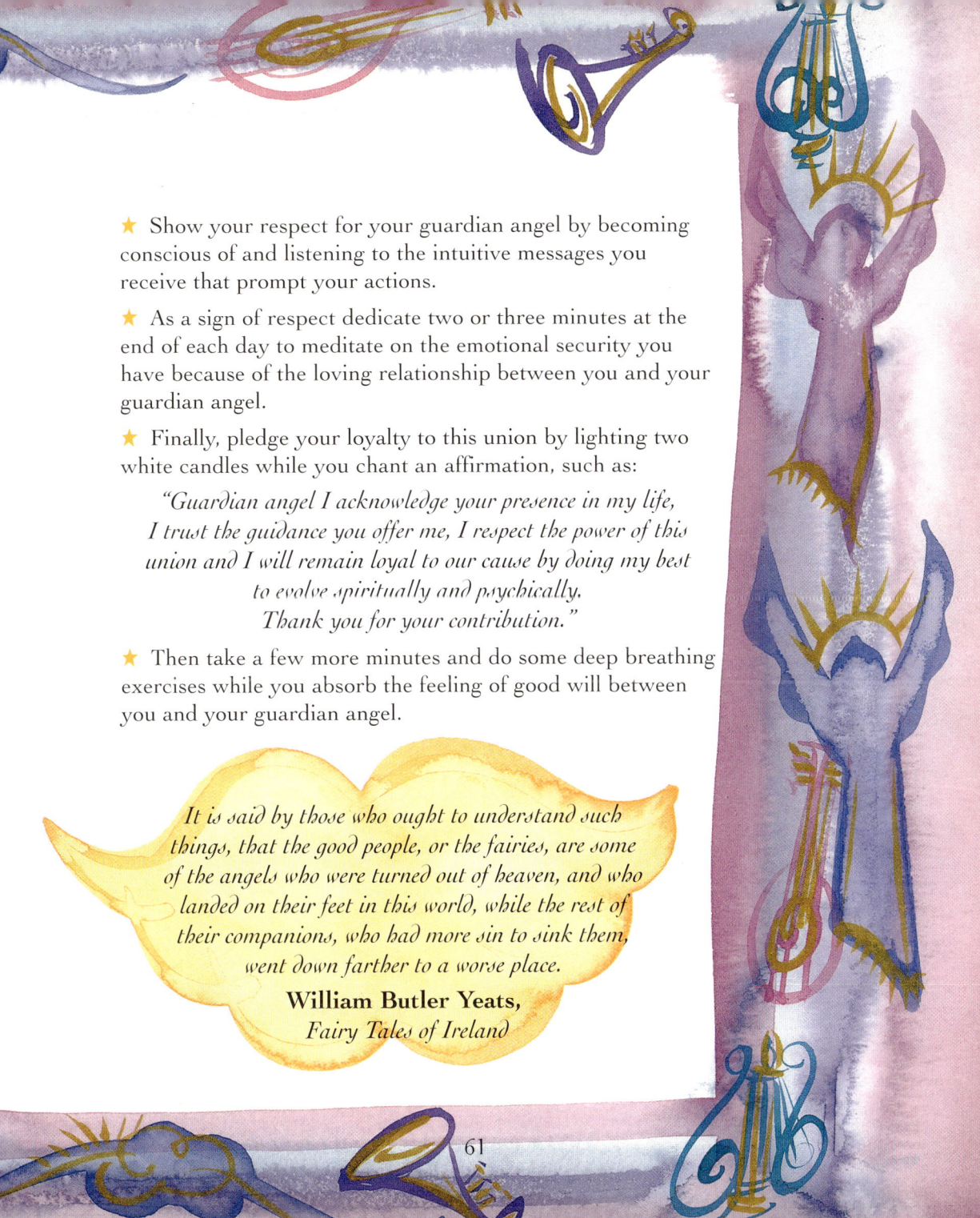

★ Show your respect for your guardian angel by becoming conscious of and listening to the intuitive messages you receive that prompt your actions.

★ As a sign of respect dedicate two or three minutes at the end of each day to meditate on the emotional security you have because of the loving relationship between you and your guardian angel.

★ Finally, pledge your loyalty to this union by lighting two white candles while you chant an affirmation, such as:

"Guardian angel I acknowledge your presence in my life, I trust the guidance you offer me, I respect the power of this union and I will remain loyal to our cause by doing my best to evolve spiritually and psychically. Thank you for your contribution."

★ Then take a few more minutes and do some deep breathing exercises while you absorb the feeling of good will between you and your guardian angel.

It is said by those who ought to understand such things, that the good people, or the fairies, are some of the angels who were turned out of heaven, and who landed on their feet in this world, while the rest of their companions, who had more sin to sink them, went down farther to a worse place.

William Butler Yeats,
Fairy Tales of Ireland

How to Communicate with Your Guardian Angel

As we have seen, guardian angels will use various methods to communicate with you (see pages 48–51). It is important to remember that your guardian angel has no wish to be intrusive and, by using methods that are effective for you, will only communicate with you if you are willing.

Using Your Intuition

Naturally for those people whose intuition and telepathic skills are heightened, either by meditation or any other consciousness-enhancing exercises or by psychic training, the guardian angel's job is made much easier. The following is a common example of how your guardian angel might use your intuition to guide you.

You have been invited to a social event, but you are not keen to go, perhaps because you don't like the people whom you believe will be there, or perhaps you are feeling low in energy. However, by afternoon you are feeling actual excitement and you then decide to go. You arrive and find that among the guests there is someone to whom you feel drawn. You are introduced and the result is that this person becomes an important part of your destiny.

How to Enhance Your Intuition

Communicating with your guardian angel through intuition is easy to achieve if you exercise your intuitive powers regularly. Form a habit of meditating for half an hour each day in a suitable atmosphere, such as your favorite room; light six white candles to represent your six senses (intuition is your sixth sense); play some relaxing music, and think of all the things your intuition tried to tell you to do during the day, then ask yourself the following questions:

★ How many times did I listen and act on the message?
★ What was the result?
★ Which intuitive messages did I ignore?
★ What was the cost?

Create a journal and record your successes and failures in detail. You will discover some fascinating facts about yourself and your progress.

Using Dream

Dream is a wonderful way to have conscious communication with your guardian angel. Whenever you want to seek specific advice from your guardian angel on any matter that is important to you, make the decision to have a meeting with your guardian angel while you sleep. Some people will be successful right away, while others may need to practice conscious dreaming for a while before they remember a meeting.

If you have difficulty remembering your dreams, try keeping a journal or notebook beside your bed and record any fragments you can remember immediately upon awakening — even if you are half asleep. This way, you will train yourself to remember dreams, and will soon develop the knack of conscious dreaming. Do not become anxious at any time, because anxiety or desperation will block any chance of success — relaxation is of the utmost importance.

Before you go to sleep create the right mood by spending half an hour in meditation. Clear your mind of all the everyday things that have bothered you, and think only of the meeting between you and your guardian angel. Now lie comfortably in your bed and imagine that you are being led by a white light to a beautiful space, and say the words:

"This is my moment, my time of great joy
My time of dreaming which nought shall annoy
Guardian angel stay close by my side
Be my companion, my staff and my guide."

And don't forget to record your dreams in detail as soon as you wake up.

Exercises to Help You Communicate with Your Guardian Angel

When communicating with your guardian angel, it is both important and rewarding to develop your own system of exercises. Simplicity and sincerity are the main components in gaining a continuous flow of communication with your guardian angel.

Affirmations that are easily committed to memory are a good way to acknowledge your guardian angel and express your desire to work with it, so that you may listen, learn and be guided by its advice in times of confusion and important life-altering decisions. Affirmations are also a wonderful way to show your guardian angel your appreciation for all that it is doing for you.

Taking the trouble to create affirmations, such as the one below, and then vocalizing them during a specific time each day, will reap untold rewards from your guardian angel, because in this way you are displaying respect.

"Guardian angel, who takes care of me in good times and in bad, who tries to dissuade me from foolish choices, and who consoles me when I'm sad, I wish to say thank you for choosing me to watch over and protect. May I gain the wisdom to know that your advice must be used for good cause and effect."

Another exercise you could use is a simple and happy exercise which requires a mere 30 minutes of your time each day. You will need a special room in your house, two white candles, some of your favorite inspirational music, and a stick of incense for burning. A good time for this exercise is half an hour before retiring for the night, because it tends to evoke pleasant dreams and restful sleep.

Begin this exercise by lighting the incense and turning on the music. As you light the first candle chant these words and imagine a white light of protection surrounding you:

"This is the candle of hope which I dedicate to you my guardian angel as a sign of the trust I place in our relationship."

64

As you light the second candle chant these words:

"This is the candle of inspiration which signifies my sincere intent to listen to the wisdom, the good judgment, and valuable guidance of my guardian angel."

Proceed by sitting or kneeling in the position that is most comfortable for you and begin some deep breathing as you absorb the music, fragrance and relaxed atmosphere that you have now created for yourself and your guardian angel.

Imagine yourself inviting the presence of your angel into your lighted circle and welcome it with respect and honor as you would your closest friend.

When visualizing your angel, allow your mind to take in detail of its appearance. For instance, does your angel have wings? Is your angel dressed in a specific way or holding a particular object? Refer to the chapter ANGELS THROUGH TIME on pages 14–31 which deals with the angels of different cultures. You may find information about your angel here, and this would give you a clue as to a spiritual path you may wish to investigate.

Sit comfortably and imagine holding your angel's hands. Feel the connection warm your soul, and vocalise your affirmations. Now concentrate on any happenings in which you had a choice to either accept them as they were or change them and discuss out loud with your guardian angel the consequences of your actions.

Conclude by thanking your guardian angel for its contribution and by chanting a short final affirmation.

"Now I am at peace with my day in the happy knowledge that, through the guidance of my guardian angel, I have done the best that I could do and been the best that I could be."

Extinguish the burning candles and incense and make special note of the dreams you have that night. Investigate further affirmation exercises, in particular see pages 70–71.

Angel Magic

Angel magic is the most potent of all the magical arts. It has been practiced by the great magicians from at least as far back as 5,000 years ago in Chaldea in Babylonia right through to the Middle Ages, the Renaissance and the nineteenth and twentieth centuries of Europe. Angel magic is the art of controlling angels, demons or fairies for the purpose of learning their secrets and exploiting their supernatural powers. Magical weapons are vital to the protection of the magician, and power is generated by incantations that consist of specific and precise words, especially those that are the secret names of God, for it is believed that to know the true name of something is to have complete control over it.

The ancient Egyptians incorporated astrology and the use of mysterious names into their angel magic, and believed that the angels could be manifested within statues, images, dreams, animals or corpses. The angel magic of the ancient Hebrews was formal and made use of weapons, prayers, oaths and incantations. The magician would wear a crown inscribed with YHVH (God's name) and a robe embroidered with magical symbols that represented the universe.

In the late sixteenth century, a scholar, Dr. John Dee, astrologer to Queen Elizabeth I, experimented through a medium named Edward Kelly with methods of contacting the world of spirits and angels. Kelly claimed that he could summon spirits by scrying (seeing images form) in a crystal or a mirror. Dee recorded the various techniques used to speak with the spirits. During the sessions, the spirits, through Kelly, were able to spell out a message. Kelly advised dictating the message backward, claiming that uncontrollably dangerous forces would be unleashed if the message were directly dictated.

Eventually Kelly and Dee claimed that they discovered a secret language called Enochian, the letters of which corresponded with numerical values, the four elements of earth, air, fire and water, and the planets. The system of Enochian magic today involves practitioners seeking a higher plane of being by using the right Enochian incantation to the appropriate angel guarding that plane.

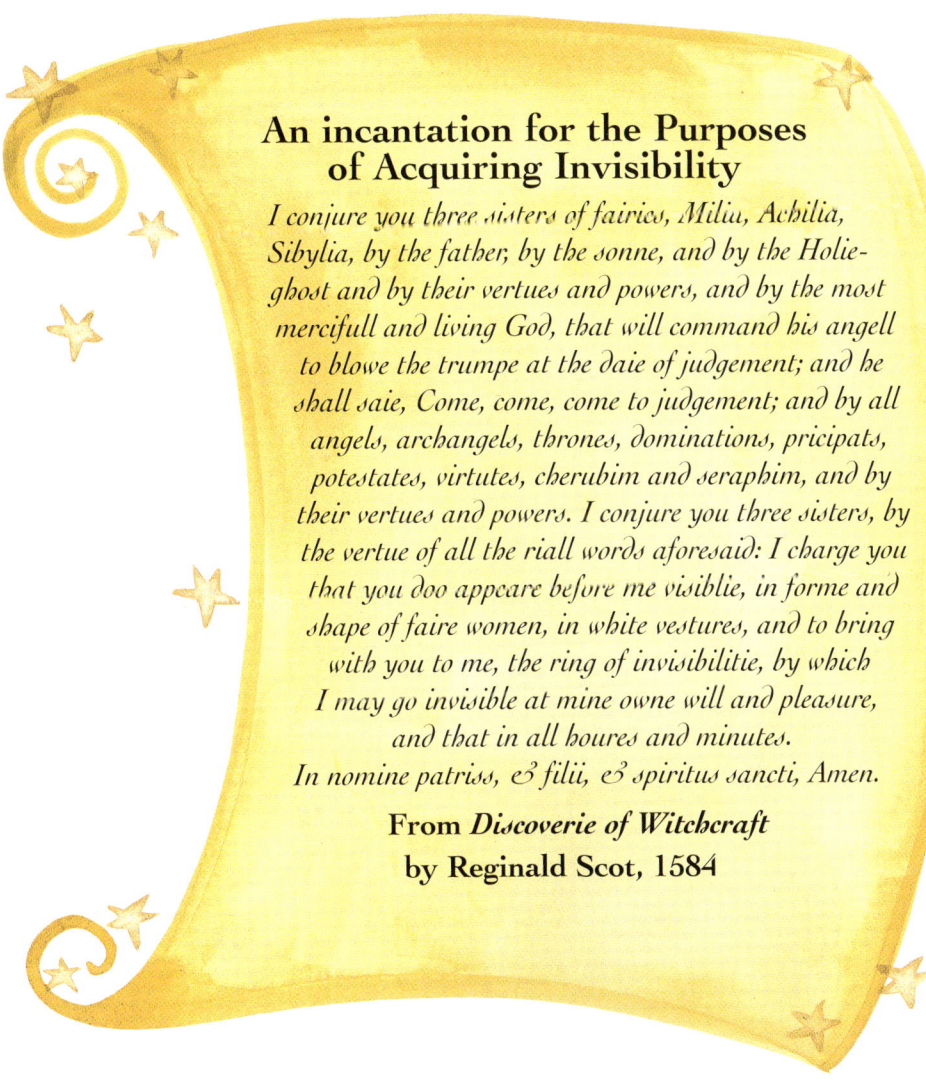

An incantation for the Purposes of Acquiring Invisibility

I conjure you three sisters of fairies, Milia, Achilia, Sibylia, by the father, by the sonne, and by the Holie-ghost and by their vertues and powers, and by the most mercifull and living God, that will command his angell to blowe the trumpe at the daie of judgement; and he shall saie, Come, come, come to judgement; and by all angels, archangels, thrones, dominations, pricipats, potestates, virtues, cherubim and seraphim, and by their vertues and powers. I conjure you three sisters, by the vertue of all the riall words aforesaid: I charge you that you doo appeare before me visiblie, in forme and shape of faire women, in white vestures, and to bring with you to me, the ring of invisibilitie, by which I may go invisible at mine owne will and pleasure, and that in all houres and minutes.
In nomine patriss, & filii, & spiritus sancti, Amen.

**From *Discoverie of Witchcraft*
by Reginald Scot, 1584**

67

Learning to Respect Your Guardian Angel

Guardian angels work tirelessly to help us with our karmic lessons. They try to encourage us to accept that which we cannot change by giving us grace and courage. Even when they know why we must endure various challenges, they try to instill in us faith and belief that there is a plan for each of us that is sometimes difficult to understand. Unfortunately, their role in our lives is often a thankless task, because we are not all born with the gifts of tolerance and patience. These are qualities which must be learned by most of us. Our guardian angels try to show us how.

Our guardian angels will always try to teach us spiritual lessons by giving us opportunities and the means through which we may learn. This does not mean that we are always willing to benefit from this valuable spiritual resource. We will be much more open to our guardian angel's help if we decide to acknowledge its valuable input and show our gratitude whenever we can. Affirmations such as the one below are appreciated by our guardian angel, because these statements confirm that we are listening to its advice and trying to learn.

"Thank you for your tolerance and for your understanding
Especially when I seem ungrateful and demanding
Teach me to appreciate the things you do for me
Let me show respect by being all that I can be."

Your guardian angel will never become tired or bored by these messages of respect and gratitude because they keep the line of communication open. Another sign of affection and respect would be to give your guardian angel a name and perhaps wear a guardian angel pin with the name engraved on it.

Your guardian angel can become your most loyal and best friend without taking the place of a human relative or friend. They only wish to intervene not intrude.

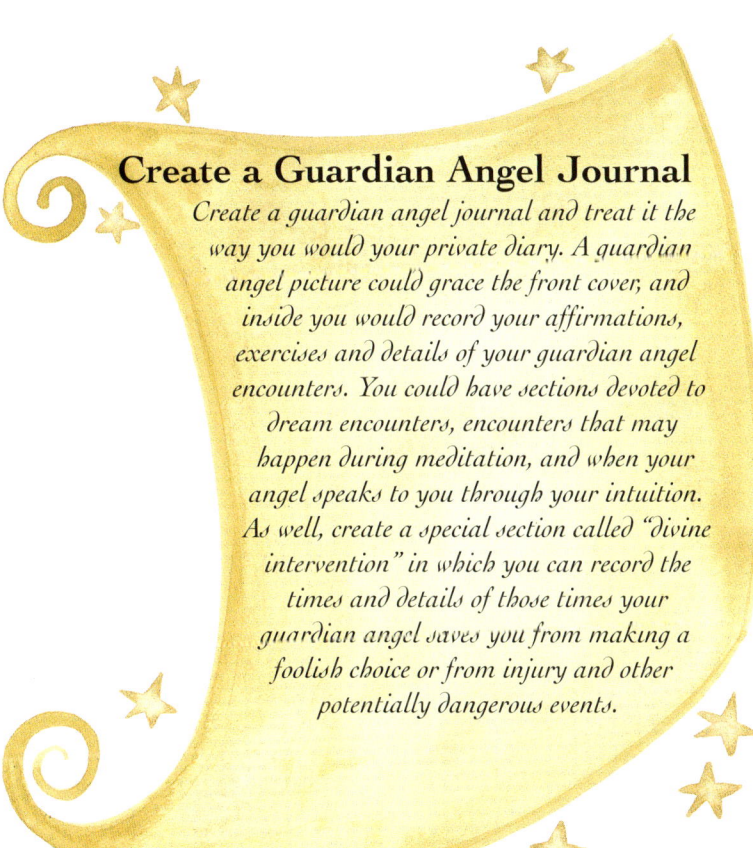

Create a Guardian Angel Journal

Create a guardian angel journal and treat it the way you would your private diary. A guardian angel picture could grace the front cover, and inside you would record your affirmations, exercises and details of your guardian angel encounters. You could have sections devoted to dream encounters, encounters that may happen during meditation, and when your angel speaks to you through your intuition. As well, create a special section called "divine intervention" in which you can record the times and details of those times your guardian angel saves you from making a foolish choice or from injury and other potentially dangerous events.

Affirmations of Respect and Protection for Your Guardian Angel

Affirmations which demonstrate acceptance and recognition of the important roles guardian angels play in our lives can become a vital part of developing and maintaining our relationship with our guardian angel. Below are two exercises you can practice that will increase the power of your affirmations.

Exercise 1

This exercise requires a positive and serene attitude and an ambience which complements the occasion. This can be achieved by lighting two white candles which represent the white light of protection that will flow between you and your guardian angel. Some relaxing mood music and an oil burner or a bowl of hot water into which you pour seven drops of essential oil will relax the atmosphere. Breathe in and out slowly until you are relaxed and then breathe normally. Now meditate on your guardian angel's presence. When you are ready, chant the following affirmation three times:

"I recognize and appreciate my guardian angel, and I do pledge to accept the guidance and listen to the advice of this divine messenger."

Exercise 2

To ensure that you are not bothered by the intervention of unwanted entities, the following affirmation will deter their interference. Follow the instructions of the first example then chant this affirmation three times:

"I fiercely reject all negative and mischievous energy from this meeting. Be gone from this place. So mote it be."

Below are more affirmations you can use to increase your bond with your guardian angel.

*"There are times when I'm lost and cannot find
The courage faith and love
To overcome the doubts and fears
Which I must rise above*

But I know when your loving arms stretch out
To guard and comfort me
I can place my feeble hand in yours
And then I will be free."

"Mystical angel who stays by my side
Through chapters of my life
I recognise and trust your hand
Protecting me from strife."

Conclusion

Now that we have a greater understanding of how angels have made themselves known to us and to other cultures across the globe and through time, we can hone our own skills in communicating with the angels that guide our destinies. As we become more accustomed to communicating with our guardian angels, we look forward to some day being able to see them through our human eyes. Our guardian angels are there to help, protect and guide us through every chapter of our lives. This is their unselfish commitment to us, which, if recognized, appreciated and respected, will ensure that we can be proud that we have lived the best lives we can. If through the wisdom of our guardian angel's guidance we are able to see the difficult periods as lessons and the lessons as blessings, then we will have achieved our goals.

Here is a message you can give to your guardian angel:

"Thank you for your unfailing support and intervention
in my life, and for your encouragement to successfully
complete the karmic lessons of my destiny. Through you
and with you, my efforts will not be in vain."

Glossary

Abraham: Old Testament. Founder of the Hebrew people, father of Isaac.

Aeon: an immeasurably long period of time; an age.

Affirmation: a statement of intent as a focus for meditation or other psychic-enhancing exercise or a form of mild self-hypnosis.

Ahura Mazda: the Wise Lord or God in Zoroastrianism.

Ancestor worship: religion based on the belief that the ancestors can influence the affairs of the living.

Ancestors: venerated deceased members of family, tribe or group that are believed to be able to influence the affairs of the living.

Angels: 9th and lowest order of angels. Includes guardian angels and all other classes of worker angels.

Animism: the belief that spirits inhabit land forms, trees, rivers, any other natural object and the cosmos. Believed to be the original religion of humankind.

Anthropomorphization: the attribution of human characteristics to animals, plants, gods, landforms or any other animate or inanimate object that is not human.

Annunciation: the announcement of the incarnation of Christ by the archangel Gabriel to Mary.

Archangels: 8th highest order of angels, but each one is in charge of all the other orders of angels.

Asha Vahishta: Zoroastrian angel of Justice and Truth.

Asparas: an equivalent to angels in Hinduism. They are female and are dancers. Counterpart to male ghandarvas.

Avalokiteshvara: the Lotus Bearer, the most loved and powerful bodhisattva of Mahayana Buddhism.

Azrael: Islam's Angel of Death.

Azazel: chief of lower demons in Judaism.

Beelzebub: Lord of the Flies.

Bodhisattvas: Sanskrit word meaning: "whose being or essence is enlightenment". Can be in either celestial or human form, has achieved perfection, yet chooses to participate in the sorrows of the world. Buddhist equivalent to angels.

Brahma: aspect of the Supreme Lord in Hinduism.

Celestial: of the heavens.

Chaldea: an ancient region of Babylonia; the land between the Euphrates delta, the Persian Gulf and the Arabian desert.

Chaldeans: ancient Semitic people who controlled southern Babylonia from the eighth to the seventh centuries B.C.

Cherub: term applied to Christianized winged baby angel. Also singular of the cherubim.

Cherubim (sing. cherub): order of angels second in rank to the seraphim. Guardians of God's glory and bearers of His throne.

Cupid: term applied to Roman winged baby angel.

Daimon: the ancient Greek concept of a guardian spirit.

Devas: Sanskrit meaning "shining ones". In Hinduism and Buddhism a divine being or god. In the West the term is given to high orders of nature angels. They are in charge of nature spirits.

Dominions: 4th highest order of angels.

Enoch: eldest son of Cain and father of Methuselah. Said to have been taken up by God physically at the end of his earthly life.

Ezekiel: Old Testament prophet.

Fravartis: guardian angels in the religion of Zoroastrianism.

Gabriel: archangel in Judeo-Christian religion. The messenger. Governing angel of the 9th Sefira of the Tree of Life. Was counselor to Joshua and Daniel.

Ghandarvas: an equivalent to angels in Hinduism. They are male and are musicians. Counterpart to female asparas.

Guardian angels: angels assigned to each person at birth by God to care for his or her spiritual and material well-being.

Hafaza: guardian angels of Islam.

Haniel: governing angel of the 7th Sefira of the Tree of Life. Transported Enoch to heaven.

Intuition: a feeling within you that tells you when something is right or wrong about a situation, thing, person or place.

Isaac: an Old Testament patriarch, son of Abraham and Sarah and father of Jacob and Esau.

Israfil: 1st angel created by Allah.

Jibra'il: Islam's equivalent of the archangel Gabriel.

Joan of Arc: (1412–1431) simple French peasant girl who led the French army to victory against the British during the Hundred Years War. Was canonized by the Catholic Church in 1920.

Kabbala: ancient Jewish mystical tradition.

Khshathra Vairya: Zoroastrian angel of Desirable Dominion or Heaven.

Koran: sacred book of Islam believed to have been dictated to Mohammed by the archangel Gabriel.

Krishna: most important aspect of the Supreme Lord in Hinduism.

Kwan Yin: female representation of the bodhisattva Avalokiteshvara in China.

Kwannon: female representation of the bodhisattva Avalokiteshvara in Japan.

Leviathan: monster of evil, female sea-dragon, great whale, crooked serpent.

Light, the: the Supreme Being, God, source of all love.

Lilith: Satan's bride and Adam's first wife.

Lucifer: the fallen Light Bearer.

Mahayana Buddhism: Buddhism of Tibet, China and Japan.

Malik: Islam's righteous angel in charge of the Muslim hell.

Metatron: governing angel of the 1st Sefira of the Tree of Life. Angel closest to God and was once Enoch.

Michael: archangel in Judeo-Christian religion. Warrior leader of the seraphim and governing angel of the 6th Sefira of the Tree of Life.

Mika'il: 2nd angel created by Allah. Equivalent to the archangel Michael.

Mohammed: (570–632) Arab prophet and founder of Islam.

Monotheism: worship of or belief in only one god.

Muse: a goddess that inspires a creative artist.

Nature spirits: includes fairies, elves, and other spirit entities that care for nature.

New Testament: the collection of writings composed soon after Christ's death and added to the Old Testament to form the Christian Bible.

Old Testament: collection of books comprising the scriptures of the Hebrew people. First part of the Bible.

Plato: (c.427 B.C. c.347 B.C.) Greek philosopher, pupil of Socrates and teacher of Aristotle. Plato is regarded as the father of Western philosophy.

Polytheism: worship of or belief in more than one god.

Powers: 6th highest order of angels.

Principalities: 7th highest order of angels.

Putti: (sing. putto) all winged baby angels in Italian art.

Pythagorus: (c.580–c.500 B.C.) Greek philosopher and mathematician. Student of Zoroaster.

Rahab: demon of chaos and angel of insolence and pride.

Raphael: archangel in Judeo-Christian religion. God's helper and in charge of guardian angels. Governing angel of the 8th Sefira of the Tree of Life. Was counselor to Isaac.

Raziel: governing angel of the 2nd Sefira of the Tree of Life. Wisdom personified.

Renaissance: the period in history that marked the end of the Middle Ages and began the modern world, beginning in Italy in the fourteenth century.

Samael: governing angel of the 5th Sefira of the Tree of Life. Leader of 12,000 angels of destruction. Angel of Death.

Sandalphon: twin brother of Metatron and originally the prophet Elias. He is the Guardian Angel of Earth and is involved in a ceaseless battle with Samael.

Satan: archdemon and Christ's enemy.

Sefirot: the ten stages of the universe that was called into being by ten utterances of God. Each Sefira represents one of the ten Divine Attributes.

Seraphim (sing. seraph): highest order of angels and guardians of God's throne. They are known as the "burning ones".

Shaman: priest or medicine man (sometimes woman) of tribal groups who intercedes with the spirits for the well-being of his or her tribe.

Shamanism: religion of certain tribal peoples based on the belief that the world is controlled by good and evil spirits that can be influenced by a shaman.

Shiva: aspect of the Supreme Lord in Hinduism.

Socrates: (c.470 B.C.–399 B.C.) Greek philosopher and teacher of Plato.

Spenta Armaiti: Zoroastrian angel of Beneficent Devotion.

Spenta Mainyu: Zoroastrian angel, Holy Spirit. An aspect of Ahura Mazda or God.

Thrones: 3rd highest order of angels.

Torah: the Pentateuch (the first five books of the Old Testament).

Tree of Life: the icon of the Kabbala that is the image of Divine balance of which all existence is a reflection.

Uriel: archangel in Judeo-Christian religion. Light of God, angel of prophecy and interpretation.

Virtues: 5th highest order of angels.

Vishnu: aspect of the Supreme Lord in Hinduism.

Vohu Manah: Zoroastrian angel of Righteous Thinking.

Zadkiel: governing angel of the 4th Sefira of the Tree of Life. Was Abraham's counselor.

Zaphkiel: governing angel of the 3rd Sefira of the Tree of Life. Angel of Contemplation.

Zoroaster: (c.628 B.C.–c.551 B.C.) founder of Zoroastrianism. Teacher of Pythagorus.

Zoroastrianism: ancient Persian religion that was the forerunner of Western religion.

Bibliography

Æ (George Russell). *The Candle of Vision*. New York: University Books, 1965.

Bloom, Pamela (ed.) *On the Wings of Angels*. Kansas City: Ariel Books, Andrews and McMeel, 1995.

Briggs, Katherine. *A Dictionary of Fairies*. London: Penguin Books, 1977.

Brown, Peter. *The Cult of the Saints*. London: The University of Chicago Press, 1981.

Campbell, Joseph. *The Hero With a Thousand Faces*. 2d ed. Princeton: Princeton University Press, 1968.

——with Moyes, Bill. *The Power of Myth*. New York: Doubleday, 1988.

Dante Alighieri. *The Vision or Hell, Purgatory, and Paradise*. Translated by Henry Francis Cary. Oxford Edition. London: Oxford University Press, 1923.

Davidson, Gustav. *A Dictionary of Angels*. New York: The Free Press, 1967, 1971.

Ferguson, John. *An Illustrated Encyclopaedia of Mysticism and the Mystery Religions*. London: Thames & Hudson, 1976.

Findhorn Community. *The Findhorn Garden*. New York: Harper & Row, 1975.

Halevi, Z'ev ben Shimon. Kabbalah: *Tradition of hidden knowledge*. London: Thames & Hudson, 1979.

Hawken, Paul. *The Magic of Findhorn*. London: Fontana, 1976.

Hillman, James. *The Soul's Code: In Search of Character and Calling*. New York: Random House, 1996.

Hinnells, John R., *Persian Mythology*. 2d ed. London: Hamlyn, 1985.

Hodson, Geoffrey. *Man's Supersensory and Spiritual Powers*. London: The Theosophical Publishing House, 1969.

—— *Occult Powers in Nature and in Man*. London: The Theosophical Publishing House, 1973.

—— *Through the Gateway of Death*. London: The Theosophical Publishing House, 1967.

Humann, Harvey, *The Many Faces of Angels*. Marina del Rey: DeVorss & Co., 1986.

James, Geoffrey. *Angel Magic*. St. Paul: Llewellyn Publications, 1995.

Leadbeater, C.W. *The Astral Plane*. London: The Theosophical Publishing House, 1933.

—— *Invisible Helpers*. 3d ed. London: The Theosophical Publishing Society, 1912.

Moody, Raymond A. *Life After Life*. New York: Bantam/Mockingbird, 1976.
—— *Reflections on Life After Life*. New York: Bantam/Mockingbird, 1977.
Nagel, Alexander. "Cherubs", *Cherubs Angels of Love*. New York: Packaged Goods Incorporated, 1994.
Payne, Phoebe D. and Bendit, Laurence J. *The Psychic Sense*. Wheaton, Ill.: Quest Book, The Theosophical Publishing House, 1970.
Ronner, John. *Know Your Angels*. Murfreesboro TN: Mamre Press, 1993.
Steiner, Rudolf. *Spiritual Guidance of Man and Humanity*. New York: Anthroposophic Press, 1950.
Wilson, Peter Lamborn, *Angels*. London: Thames and Hudson, 1980.
Zaehner, R.C., *Hinduism*. London: Oxford University Press,1962.

Articles

"Ancient Middle Eastern Religions: A Survey of Ancient Middle Eastern Religions: Ancient Iranian religions." Britannica CD 99 Multimedia Edition 1994–1999 Encyclopaedia Britannica, Inc.
"Joan of Arc." Ibid.
"Religious Doctrines and Dogmas: Major Themes and Motifs: Angels and Demons." Ibid.
"Systems of Religious and Spiritual Belief: Ancestor Worship: Ancestor worship in religions of the world." Ibid.
"Systems of Religious and Spiritual Belief: Animism: The Animistic World View." Ibid.
"Systems of Religious and Spiritual Belief: Forms of Polytheistic Powers, Gods, and Demons." Ibid.

Web Sites

Catholic Online. http://saints.catholic.org
Near Death Experience Research Foundation. http://www.ndef.org
International Association for Near Death Studies (IANDS). http://www.iands.org
Dr. Melvin Morse. http://www.melvinmorse.com
Dr. Raymond Moody. http://www.lifeafterlife.com
The Findhorn Foundation and Community. http://www.findhorn.org

index

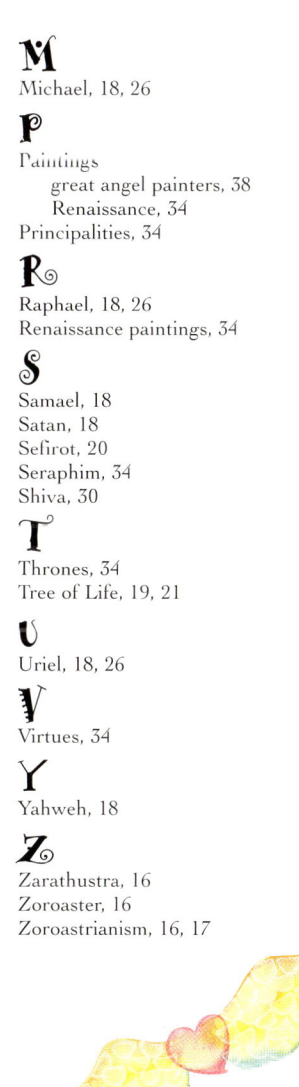

First published by Lansdowne Publishing Pty Ltd, 1999

This edition published in 2000 by
Parkgate Books
London House
Great Eastern Wharf
Parkgate Road
London SW11 4NQ
Great Britain

1 3 5 7 9 8 6 4 2

British Library Cataloguing-in-Publication Data:
A catalogue record for this book is available from the British Library.

ISBN 1 902616 96 0

Designer: Sylvie Abecassis
Cover illustration: Penny Lovelock
Illustrator: Joanna Davies

Set in Cochin on QuarkXPress
Printed in Singapore by Tien Wah Press (Pte) Ltd